Heritage of Faith

A Framework for Whole Community Catechesis

Heritage of Faith

A Framework for Whole Community Catechesis

Jo McClure Rotunno

The Scripture passages contained herein are from the *New Revised Standard Version of the Bible*, copyright © 1989, by the Division of Christian Education of the National Council of Churches in the U.S.A. All rights reserved.

Twenty-Third Publications
A Division of Bayard
185 Willow Street
P.O. Box 180
Mystic, CT 06355
(860) 536-2611 or (800) 321-0411
www.twentythirdpublications.com
ISBN:1-58595-309-1

Copyright ©2004 Jo McClure Rotunno. All rights reserved. No part of this publication may be reproduced in any manner without prior written permission of the publisher. Write to the Permissions Editor.
Printed in the U.S.A.

Contents

INTRODUCTION 1

CHAPTER 1 Next Steps for Parish Catechesis **5**

CHAPTER 2 Catechesis for the Whole Community of Faith **16**

CHAPTER 3 A Model for Whole Community Catechesis **26**

CHAPTER 4 Year A: Questions of the Week **36**

CHAPTER 5 Year B: Questions of the Week **62**

CHAPTER 6 Year C: Questions of the Week **87**

CHAPTER 7 Session Theme Outlines for Year A **113**

Introduction

This is a small book about a big idea—whole community catechesis. This intergenerational approach, widely discussed and advocated by Bill Huebsch over the past few years, may offer the best opportunity yet for drawing together all ages and stages of a parish community into a faith journey of ongoing learning and conversion.

Over the past several years, as I have listened to the concerns of pastors, DREs, and diocesan staff about the state of their local catechetical programs, I have heard one overarching concern. All are convinced that families today urgently need help from the parish to clarify what it means to be faithful Catholics in today's complex world. Families need guidance in appreciating their church's doctrinal and biblical heritage, as well as to see practical connections between that faith tradition and life.

Somehow the present delivery system is not working. A strong case can still be made for a children's curriculum organized by grade or age group. Children have developmental characteristics that make a peer-group approach very useful in their faith development. But this needs to be augmented by intergenerational gatherings that also allow them to learn from (and contribute to!) the wisdom of the whole community. They also need vivid liturgical experiences and practical opportunities to participate in works of charity and justice.

As the intergenerational approach is being discussed more widely, many are looking for resources and ideas to help them organize this style of catechesis in their parishes. John Roberto, with his *Generations of Faith* approach, has probably done the most so far to organize a doctrinal scope and sequence on an intergenerational structure. As with any big new idea, many other persons will continue to discuss and refine what organizing principles should guide this new catechetical form. The chapters that follow are meant as one more contribution to that ongoing conversation.

Another Approach

The parish event attended by the greatest number of parishioners is the Sunday liturgy, without doubt the most teachable moment for all who are present. Over a three-year cycle, the Sunday lectionary provides a systematic approach to the church's biblical heritage, centered on the life and ministry of Jesus Christ. But the church also has a 2000-year doctrinal tradition rooted in the Scriptures to be sure but also organized in its own categories of theological reflection. My approach is to try and wed these two traditions in a way that honors the wisdom of each.

I call this approach a "double-spiral" approach. It follows the sequence of themes addressed by the seasons of the liturgical cycle. But it merges the seasonal lectionary with a series of six doctrinal themes that will repeat—in the same sequence but with new emphases—each year of the three-year cycle. Chapter 7 of this book will take Year A of the lectionary cycle and offer an example of how this double-spiral approach could work.

About This Book

First, a few words about what this book is not. It does not offer you a complete curriculum. It is not a handbook, telling you in a comprehensive way what to do and how to do it. It is not a complete path to whole community catechesis. It is an example of how a scope and sequence of themes for parish-wide faith reflection might begin. Rather than waiting and presenting you with the finished product, I would rather seek the widest possible consultation with those of you at the grass roots level. As you respond to what you read here, your insights will help us know where to take this next.

I believe there is enough given here to help some of you pick up the idea and test it out. If you do, I hope you will get in touch and give us your feedback. We do intend to work toward a published resource to support whole community catechesis, and we'd love to include your insights in the final form of the product.

A Final Note

With the encouragement of Bill Huebsch, I have written the first three chapters of this book in the "plain English" style he has popularized. I have found his style of writing to be helpful in my own teaching. I hope I have done it justice in the pages that follow.

Most of all, I hope that this little book will provide a small but useful step in the ongoing conversation on what it means to build a vibrant, learning community of faith. I hope it will help you discover better ways of gathering adults and children of all ages and inviting them to share faith and knowledge together. My goal is to inspire children and the adult community to enter into a lifelong journey of faith formation.

CHAPTER 1

Next Steps for Parish Catechesis

My first year as a religious educator was in 1968
in a third grade classroom in Los Angeles.
Since I had graduated from a Catholic college,
I somehow was considered qualified
to assist in the religious formation of eight-year-olds.
I gamely developed lesson plans,
leading bored youngsters through the etymology
of words like Eucharist and reconciliation.
They were interested, though only momentarily,
to learn that the words
reconciliation and eyelash share the same Latin root!
Many of my classes inspired the familiar answer to
"What did you learn in religion class today?"
"Nothing much."
I'm sure the children's thoughts were on recess and the lunch menu,
as mine had been at their age,
when answers to *Baltimore Catechism* questions
droned on, up one aisle and down the other.

College theology notwithstanding,
I had no experience in adult religious formation,
much less catechist formation.

Fortunately for the children and for me,
a life-altering event occurred the next year.
When my son was six, I entered him into
the CCD program at our parish.
The pastor asked two questions about my background,
flashed a big Irish smile,
and handed me a fourth grade catechist guide.
"With your wonderful experience," he said,
"I know you'll be willing to do your part
for our religion program."

These were the first true post-Vatican II textbooks
I had seen.
I could see that the language of theology
had changed from my college years,
and the catechist background pages in the guides
were my teaching "bible" for a year or two.
I followed the lesson plans carefully,
and gradually learned by doing
how to help kids make connections
between doctrine and their life experience.
Like many of my peers,
I probably gave them too many balloons and banners
in those heady days of the early '70s,
but I know I witnessed the love of God to them
and helped them experience
a welcoming community of faith.

I began to take advantage of short adult education classes
offered at my parish by Vincentian priests
from the nearby diocesan seminary.
At the same time, a patient DRE
pushed and prodded me to do more.
I began to attend area workshops
and the Los Angeles Religious Education Congress.

Eventually, I entered a process
of catechist formation in the diocese.
This was the shining moment for me,
the first opportunity I had had
to reflect on my personal faith journey
in a community of catechists,
and to explore in a systematic way
the teachings of Vatican II.
From that year forward, I was hooked.
Assisting in the faith formation of others
would become a lifelong work.

A Different Day

In many ways, however,
we now live in different times.
As with all moments of social, intellectual, and spiritual upheaval,
the first wave of excitement
that followed upon the fresh ideas of the Council
has passed.
The pendulum has swung back to the center
and, some would say, too far to the right.
But it is a predictable moment in religious history,
similar to what sociologists of religion call
the "institutionalization of charism."

Karl Rahner and Pope John XXIII are gone.
We are now taking the charismatic moment of the Council,
when the depth of theological insight
and simplicity of mission
were embraced by the Church,
and doing the hard work of applying
the profound truths of the Council
to our local situations
and to yet newer signs of the times.
Today we are engaged in the difficult task
of finding a balance and a better delivery system.

On the one hand, we still recognize
the immediacy of God's presence
in our everyday experience.
We want to help others
name it,
reflect on it,
and celebrate it.
But we also want budding disciples to know
the richness of our Scriptures and tradition,
and the ways these two sources
can deepen their understanding of experience,
just as this heritage has enriched our own.

Beyond Childhood

Many of the innovations in religious education materials
have focused on the needs of children,
and necessarily so.
The church has no greater responsibility
than to pass on the heritage of faith to the young
in ways that lead to a more profound conversion.
But from the documents of Vatican II onward,
the church has mandated
that equal attention be paid to adult formation.

Some valuable advances have been made,
the most successful and well-known of which
is currently the Rite of Christian Initiation of Adults.
In addition, many Catholic adults today
have gained a deeper appreciation
of their biblical heritage
through Bible study programs in the parish.
The Charismatic renewal led to
the formation of small parish groups
who celebrate the Spirit
and focus on prayer and Christian community.

Programs like RENEW, the Cursillo movement,
and the emergence of small faith communities
have contributed to a spiritual reawakening
among adult Catholics.
However, anyone who looks at the structure and budgets
of the majority of American parishes can see that,
almost forty years after Vatican II,
much still needs to be done for adult faith formation.
In spite of repeated statements from Rome
and from the American bishops,
adult formation is far from the center
of parish catechetical ministry.
The purpose of this book is to suggest some practical steps
that parishes can take toward the outcome called for
by the *General Directory for Catechesis* (GDC):
a "living, explicit, and fruitful" adult faith (GDC, no. 82).

A Graced Moment

The past several years have been tumultuous ones
for American society:
worldwide terrorism,
an unpredictable economy,
electronic media that often delivers
a shallow and cynical message,
a fast-paced environment that delivers or demands
instant solutions
and allows little time for silence or reflection.
The church, which should stand as a beacon of hope
in these troubled times,
has instead been ripped apart by scandal
and increased polarization
between its conservative and liberal wings.
All these elements have undermined the church's moral influence
and placed unprecedented stress
on the present form of the institution.

Yet, in the midst of all this turmoil,
the Spirit still moves.
Catechumens still gather in parishes
and wrestle with the gospel on their journey of faith.
Catechists still witness the love of Christ to the young.
Youth groups step out into their communities
on missions of charity and justice.
Faithful priests, women religious, and lay leaders
still dedicate their lives
to the continuation of the mission of Jesus.

Crises are often challenging opportunities
for the inbreaking of the Spirit.
All of us have seen examples of this in our own lives.
Our prevailing worldview is a good indicator
of how we will respond to these challenges.
In the course of my own public speaking
I have encountered two kinds of parish leaders.
The first group I call the "naysayers".
You know their message:
"It is impossible to get good catechists these days
—people have no time."
"No one comes to parent meetings anymore
unless you threaten them."
"We tried adult education one year
and only seven people showed up."

The second group—
and their numbers are growing larger and louder—
are "harbingers of hope".
Sometimes they are new DREs,
too new to be jaded by failure.
Many are experienced DREs
who never learned to take no for an answer.
But all have the temperament
to see the cup of parish life as half-full.

Even when a parent truthfully says, "I have no time,"
they see underneath that comment
a person who wishes that she or he did,
and who might make the time
if she or he thought that the parish had anything to offer
that would feed their inner hunger.

Whole Community Catechesis

For many adults, the local parish
has become irrelevant to their growth in faith.
Yet the *General Directory* reminds us that the parish is
"the most important *locus* in which the Christian community
is formed and expressed" (GDC, no. 257).
The *Directory* also recognizes
that if the parish is to be a true center of life and faith,
realistic attention to the faith needs of adults
will have to become a priority.
But how can this be done,
when so much time, talent, and treasure in parishes
is given now to children's catechesis?
Neither the personnel nor the money seems available
to add another major focus.
Quite simply,
we will always find time for whatever program or process
we consider to be most important.

Around the same time as the promulgation of the GDC,
a new idea began to crystallize
in the catechetical community.
This idea has come to be known as whole community catechesis,
the term popularized by Bill Huebsch,
a tireless advocate
for the values of the Second Vatican Council.
Bill has crisscrossed the country
encouraging DREs and pastors to step up
and do what they know in their hearts is needed—

to draw the whole parish community of faith together
in a process of faith formation.
He has found a surprising number of parishes
eager to do this.
They believe they have reached the end of the line
with their present delivery system
and are looking for a new way
to set hearts on fire with the good news.
You may work in one of these parishes—or you want to.

Bill has written books specifically on this subject.
Whole Community Catechesis in Plain English,
and a companion book:
A Handbook for Success in Whole Community Catechesis,
which give parishes a practical path
to put in place this inclusive new style of catechesis.
Whole community catechesis
gathers parishioners across the generations
into a process that is both instructional and formative.
Participants reflect on the Word,
share faith,
learn and pray together,
and enjoy the hospitality of the parish.
This process probably should not replace
core programs for children and youth.
However, it affirms the truth that the GDC states so clearly—
that the whole parish is "catechist,"
and all its members are in constant need
of deeper conversion.

Bill Huebsch suggests that all parishes
begin whole community catechesis
with a simple process based on what he calls
the Question of the Week.

It is a lectionary-based question,
usually from the Sunday gospel,
that invites reflection on the message of Jesus Christ
and leads into daily life.
If you have not yet initiated this process in your parish,
you will find sample reflection questions
for all three years of the liturgical cycle
in Chapters 4 to 6 of this book.

These Questions of the Week can be introduced
in the Sunday homily;
printed in the parish bulletin;
explored in short, small group gatherings
over coffee and donuts after Mass;
used to begin parish or school religion classes;
and incorporated, in fact, into every gathering in the parish
over the course of the week.

The Next Step

What is a next step
that can include *all* the members of the parish?
I believe that it is a process
that will allow the whole community
to begin to explore the fundamental insights
of the Catholic tradition
in innovative and friendly ways.
Ideally, it will happen in a setting
that includes whole households,
families,
single persons,
older adults,
even the disillusioned
who have migrated to the edge of parish life.
Why is it so important to move
to a more systematic approach to adult catechesis?

Because every parish leader recognizes
that the adult Catholic population
is less and less articulate about its doctrinal tradition.
Children's programs, rather than serving family faith,
often introduce dichotomies
between the faith perceptions of children and parents.
The same parents, hungry to give moral guidance
especially to their teenage children,
cannot find a language to defend
their most deeply held moral values.

Will they come?
How you name a gathering goes a long way
toward drawing the audience.
"Exploring the Seven Sacraments"
may not draw a crowd.
But call your series "Celebrations of Life"
and give the topics names like
"Learning to Ask for Forgiveness" and
"Facing Illness with Courage,"
and you might find some takers.
As a well-known movie from the last decade put it,
"If you build it,
they will come."

Sharing the Heritage of Faith

If you would prefer to cut corners
in reading this book,
you'll find the heart in Chapter 7.
Chapter 7 outlines an approach
to six doctrinal themes
that allows you to bring the whole parish together
for experiences of learning and reflection.
Your gatherings for each theme might be held
on four evenings
or on a single day in each liturgical season.

The themes are organized so that each year
you will address different topics
related to six categories of Christian doctrine:
Revelation and Faith
Jesus
Morality
Church
Paschal Mystery/Sacraments
and Mission.
The themes are connected in a unique way
to the three years of the Sunday lectionary.
The examples in this book treat themes connected to Year A.

The next chapter offers some background
on recent church thinking on adult formation.
It also suggests some beginning steps you will want to take
to help all the members
in your faith community
deepen their faith and so
find their hearts burning within them.

Questions for Discussion

- What programs and processes in your parish have helped lay the groundwork for whole community catechesis?
- Do you tend to resist or embrace change?
- What is most appealing about the idea of whole community catechesis? What is your greatest concern?

CHAPTER 2

Catechesis for the Whole Community of Faith

The goal of Christian life is
to witness the good news
so that each generation can know the Father's love
and, through the Spirit,
find salvation through Jesus Christ.
Where does this Christian faith begin?

The seed of faith is planted in us by God,
and all baptized Christians have a right and a duty
to bring this seed to maturity (GDC, 173).
The mission belongs to everyone
without exception.
The role of the church's leaders is
to equip the people of God for ministry
so that this goal may be fulfilled,
and all may live "the truth in love" (Ephesians 4:15).

We will best achieve this goal of maturing in faith
within vibrant communities of faith.

Some people ask,
"Why can't faith be a solitary journey?"
To find the answer, we only need to look
at the ministry of Jesus Christ.
Jesus' work was not done alone.
He gathered a community of disciples.
He lived among them,
taught them,
prayed with them,
and sent them out—
not alone, but "in pairs" (Luke 10:1–12).

Ideally, our first community of faith is the family,
as it was for Jesus.
In the family we first witness to
the love of God and the fellowship of Jesus Christ,
practice forgiveness,
and learn to love and serve others.
That is why parish leaders must continue
to remind themselves that their role is
to serve the family and help it grow—
not the other way around.
Catechists, especially, must serve the needs of the family,
remembering that the family is, after all,
the first catechist.

The Catholic Parish

The parish, on the other hand,
"is the Eucharistic community and the heart
of the liturgical life of Christian families;
it is a privileged place for the catechesis
of children and parents"
(CCC, 2226).
The parish initiates new members
into the fullness of Christian life.

It gathers all its members
to celebrate,
to learn,
to practice charity,
and to transform the world.
From the early centuries of the Church,
the parish has offered the gift of an assembly
praising God in one voice,
united in belief and ritual,
standing as a beacon of hope,
with hands joined to bring about the reign of God.

Because of what it signifies,
the parish is both curriculum and catechist
for the people of God.
Father Bob Hater has long supported this insight,
saying that if your catechetical program is ailing,
it is probably because
your parish is not working as well as it should.
Yet the only persons who can improve parish life
are its members,
particularly the adult community.
If the members have not been formed in faith,
they will not have the vision for the task,
and a cycle of disappointment and failure
will be the consequence.
The conclusion is a bit obvious, then.
All believers need to be about the task of building
life-giving, transforming communities of faith.
Yet this will not happen without
a "strong, systematic catechesis" for all parishioners
that nurtures ongoing conversion
(*Our Hearts Were Burning within Us*, OHWB, 3).
That is why whole community catechesis
makes so much sense.

Without doing away with existing catechetical programs
that may be working quite well,
we can occasionally begin to hold
the large intergenerational gatherings
advocated by Bill Huebsch and others.
We might begin with large seasonal assemblies
where cross-sections of the parish explore a faith theme
for an evening, a series of evenings, or a day.
We can link our reflections to the seasonal lectionary,
without following it slavishly
Sunday by Sunday.

The Primacy of Adult Faith Formation

The church has been advocating adult faith formation
since the Second Vatican Council
(*Decree on the Apostolate of the Laity*, AA, 4).
Yet even today, most parish programs,
still place their highest priority
on the faith formation of children.
With the exception of the preparation of parents
for their children's first celebration of sacraments,
or a family's entry into the church through the RCIA,
there is little connection among the catechetical initiatives
for the various stages of life.
Yet the church reminds us not to develop our programs
as "watertight compartments,"
but to make them complementary (GDC, 72).
One goal of faith formation
is to give coherence to the faith journey
through all its ages and stages.
We are all trying to construct a narrative
from the pieces of our experience.
We want to understand the story
our lives are telling now, and to foresee
what the topic for the next chapter might be.

As faith grows, our lives become increasingly centered
on Jesus and his message.
While faith can mature at an unusually early ages,
as it did with the prophet Samuel
and with Mary,
it usually takes the perspective of adulthood
for faith to reach its fullness.
Adults, as well as children and youth,
benefit from a process that allows them to explore
the great themes of Scripture and tradition—
but always in a way that will link faith and life.

What Is Faith?

Faith is personal adherence to God
and assent to his truth (CCC, 150).
As our faith matures, it becomes
"living, explicit, and fruitful" (GDC, 82).
When our faith is living,
we grow and develop,
learn from our experience,
adapt to changing circumstances,
and move through seasons.
We search for understanding,
seek forgiveness and renewal,
live the paschal mystery,
and long for eternal life.
Yet we know that our faith needs nourishment,
and we find that nourishment
through liturgy,
prayer,
the reading of the word of God,
works of justice,
and love of God and neighbor.
When our faith is explicit,
we call Jesus our Lord.

We live in a Christian community,
we relate to the communion of Persons
that is the Trinity,
and we connect with the teaching of our church.
We are confident
because we are intimate with the word of God.
We are confirmed by the faith of the church.
We rejoice in our diversity,
and believe with the church that there should be
"unity in what is necessary,
freedom in what is doubtful,
and charity in everything"
(*Pastoral Constitution on the Church in the Modern World*, GS, 92).

When our faith is fruitful,
it overflows with the Spirit's fruits
of charity, joy, and peace,
patience, kindness, and goodness,
generosity, gentleness, and faithfulness,
modesty, chastity, and self-control.
It brings compassion to all
and shares its treasure with those
in the community and beyond.
All these thoughts are gathered for us
in the excellent document of the American bishops,
Our Hearts Were Burning within Us (OHWB, 50–63).
Here they exhort us to build programs
of adult faith formation
that will support maturity of faith.
In fact, the bishops begin their document by reminding us
that adult faith formation
is the *central* task of catechesis (OHWB, 1).

Later, in reiterating the importance
of the parish community of faith,
they put it even more boldly:

"While the parish may have
an adult faith formation program,
it is no less true that the parish *is*
an adult faith formation program" (OHWB, 121).
Those who look at the hard work
of adult faith formation with trepidation
would be wise to remember the benefits.
Every church ministry will be energized
when adult faith formation is strong.
Children's programs will grow
because families will be stronger.
Youth programs will grow
because young people will be surrounded
by stronger adult role models.
Catechists will be easier to find
because they will be more confident
of their adult faith.

How Will We Begin?

As we begin to plan for whole community catechesis,
we'll bear three principles in mind.
We'll need to be aware of how the members of our community
imagine and communicate with God.
We'll want to be conscious of their degree of belief.
We'll attend to those whose faith is shaky
or who are searching,
and empower those whose faith
is truly wise and mature
to share their gifts with the community.
We will be as sensitive as possible
to the personal situations of every person
and to their moral challenges and questions.
Armed with this knowledge,
we'll invite them to deeper conversion
to the mystery and message of Jesus Christ.

We'll call them to discipleship
and encourage their active participation
in the Christian community.
We'll keep these principles in mind
as we develop our programs.

Word, Worship, and Service

Catechesis is a ministry of the word,
a moment in the process of evangelization.
However, the formation of adult faith ultimately involves
more than catechesis.
An intimate relationship and complementarity exists
among the parish's ministries
of word, worship, and service.
Only when the members of a community
are touched to their depths
by the power of good liturgy
and by acts of charity and forgiveness,
as well as by good catechesis,
will true conversion occur.

What are the implications of this?
Well, for one thing, liturgists and catechists
will need to work together
in Christian charity.
Both will need to know
what the outreach activities of the parish are—
and how to link more parishioners to them.
Each group knows the importance of its own ministry,
but will need to remember the equal importance
of the other two.
The liturgists among us will understand
the hard work others are doing
to love and serve the Lord and one another
through their own ministries.

Persons engaged in outreach ministry will understand better
the importance of silence and prayer,
reflection and celebration.
We'll all work together to give adults
a better understanding of the Church's ritual life
and an experience of Christian service.
Sometimes these changes are easier to talk about
than to accomplish.
However, accomplish them we must
for the sake of the whole faith community.

A Preferential Option

It won't be easy at first
to create a preferential option for adults
in our plans and programs.
So that faith can be handed over
with greater assurance,
we'll have to place adults
at the center of our parish's pastoral plan,
and keep reminding ourselves of our duty to serve
all the members of our parish,
especially the marginalized
who are so easy to overlook.
Sometimes it will be hard,
since our planning time is bound to converge
with the pressures of First Eucharist,
or the usual parent meetings,
or any of the many daily crises
that keep us from putting first things first.

We'll want to look to the catechumenate as a model
for all our adult formation programs.
We find in the catechumenate
proclamation of the word,
reflection and dialogue,
prayer and presentation of the mysteries of faith.

Here, adults are invited to question,
and the gradual nature of conversion is respected.
In the RCIA we welcome all who seek faith
to come as they are.
We incorporate the whole parish into the process.
We respect the cultures of our participants
and celebrate the gift of their diversity.
We celebrate their moments of growth
with rites, and biblical and liturgical signs.
Throughout the process, we surround them
with the power of the paschal mystery,
culminating in the rites of the Easter vigil.
When we can describe all parish programs
with this same language,
we will be well on the road to success.

If we wade into the waters of adult formation,
we'll find ourselves surprisingly refreshed.
The transformation of our parishes will take time—
years, in fact.
However, as we begin creating more programs
based on real questions from people's lives,
we'll be energized as we find
our parishes coming to a greater fullness of life.

Questions for Discussion

- What has been your own best experience of catechesis? Why do you remember it?
- Where do the best examples of catechesis occur in your parish?
- What first step can you take in your parish to build a catechetical program that serves the whole community of faith?

CHAPTER 3

A Model for Whole Community Catechesis

Adults in the American Catholic Church
are much harder to categorize than they might have been
in our grandparents' day,
but we can say a few things with assurance.

First, adults come to us today
from a rich variety of cultures.
Rather than being a challenge,
this diversity is a gift of inestimable value
to our local churches.
It affords so many more lenses
through which to look at
our tradition and our experience.
We have always known
that our individual images of God
were too small.
Taken together, however,
the multitude of images and world views
revealed through different cultures

enriches our understanding of God
and deepens our faith.

Second, our catechesis will be changed forever
by technology.
While dangers exist in this revolution,
It offers many more strengths.
The globalization of society
made possible by this shift to an Internet world
offers us a wider world view
than any we had imagined.
The possibilities for communication,
for learning,
for the sharing of ideas,
and for cultural understanding
are practically boundless.
Rather than fearing this revolution,
we can channel it
for the work of bringing about God's reign.

Third, a new strain of independent thinking
is alive and growing in the church,
especially among young adults.
Many of us have been surprised to learn about
the numbers of young adult Catholics
who still feel part of the Catholic tradition,
yet differ with the church
on various important teachings.
A substantial number do not feel
that marriage outside the church
is a barrier to active participation in the Eucharist.
A similarly large number have claimed
(as reported in the research of James Davidson et. al.)
that birth control and even abortion
may not be morally wrong in all cases.

Many more believe that the church would be better off
run as a democratic institution
along the lines of the American political model.
Rather than engage in the futile task
of suppressing these viewpoints,
we would be wise to allow young adults to express them,
and to enter into dialogue
with the wisdom of our tradition.
Many of these young adults
are the parents of the children in our programs.
Only by giving these challenging voices a home
will we be able to say we have gathered in
the whole community of faith.
Those who are honestly searching
will always enrich our assemblies.

Fourth, older members of our parish
need a place at the table.
Often we see them as passive
and beyond the need for more than pastoral care.
But they, too, have special catechetical needs.
They may have a strong faith but have been
the recipients of poor religious formation.
Many have been wounded spiritually,
sometimes by the church.
They are approaching the end of their earthly lives,
and have a deep need
to integrate their lifetime of faith
and to prepare for the life to come.
They need the support of the faith community.
Many among the elderly
can also be wisdom figures in our assemblies,
especially for the young.
However, they will need to be invited, acknowledged, and affirmed
by catechists and parish leaders
in order to see the riches they have to share with others.

Our invitation to them can add a deeper dimension
to intergenerational faith sharing events.

A Way to Begin

When do we gather together,
what will our curriculum be,
and how will we organize ourselves to share faith?
There are a number of prevailing models
in faith formation today.
One of the earliest new models was
a purely lectionary-based approach,
such as the *Seasons of Faith* program
which was popular for a number of years
and included materials for all generations.
It was originally designed as an alternative
to doctrinally-based curriculum.
Another model is the family-based model,
also rooted in the lectionary,
such as Kathleen Chesto's *F.I.R.E.* program.

More recently, John Roberto is advocating
an intergenerational model
called *Generations of Faith*
which is being piloted throughout the United States.
This long-term project is comprehensive in scope.
Its goal is to prepare participants of all ages
to participate more fully
in all the events of church life—
liturgical feasts and seasons,
sacramental celebrations,
and outreach activities of peace and justice,
through a process of reflection and application to life.
All these models are strong approaches with good insights
and enthusiastic supporters.

Another Way

My own suggestion is a relatively simple one.
It is rooted in a conviction that change
will need to happen a bit more slowly
in the average parish.
Children's programs,
which have been entrenched for generations,
will not, and probably should not, change quickly.
There will always be a value in offering children
a developmentally appropriate introduction to faith
that invites them to reflect and explore
within a group of their peers.
However, they also need more connections
to the wisdom of the whole faith community.

Scripture and Tradition

We also need to face
the legitimate concern within the episcopate
about the lack of adult faith formation
and begin to incorporate
a more structured scope and sequence of content
into programs that include adults.
The *New Adult Catechism* will provide direction for this.
Yet the church also recognizes
the importance of the Scriptures,
for Christian faith flies with the two wings
of Scripture and tradition.
When both are honored, our approach can create
"a symphony in which the unity of faith
finds expression in richly diverse
formulations and manifestations" (OHWB, 89).

Double-Spiral Approach

One problem with a strictly lectionary-based approach is that
the doctrinal content can be a bit "scattershot."

A better way might be to organize
the doctrinal content of the faith
both sequentially and seasonally.
We would refer to the seasonal lectionary,
    but not in a strict week-by-week correspondence.
We would offer the same doctrinal themes
    in the same sequence each year,
    but we would address different topics
        around those themes.
Support for this approach can be found
    in the three-year lectionary.
Over the course of three years,
    the parish would reflect upon
        all the core teachings of our Catholic tradition.

The example included in this book
    shows one way to begin doing this.
All new participants would begin the process
    with a fall series called "The Journey of Faith."
They would explore what it means
    to form a household of faith,
    identify their own search for God,
    learn how God speaks in Scripture and tradition,
    and learn how to use the Bible more effectively.
Beginning with Advent, the whole community would begin
    a series of explorations of simple concepts
    related to six key themes of Christian faith:
        Revelation and faith
        Jesus
        Ministry
        Morality
        Paschal Mystery
        Sacraments
        Church and Mission.

We would offer one theme
in each season of the liturgical year:
Advent: Revelation and Faith
Christmas: Jesus (Incarnation)
Ordinary Time: Jesus (Ministry)
Lent: Morality
Triduum and Easter: Paschal Mystery/Sacraments
Ordinary Time: Church and Mission

Each year, the same themes would be explored once again
in a spiral sequence, but with new topics
grounded in the new year's lectionary.
In such a model, the richness of the seasonal lectionary
would be honored,
but the themes of Catholic doctrine
would begin to have more coherence.

A Way to Gather

Such a model can be used in a variety of settings:
large intergenerational assemblies,
family clusters,
small communities of faith,
or even traditional adult study groups—
to name the most likely ways we could gather.
Groups can gather
for an evening,
a series of evenings,
or a day of reflection
in each liturgical season.
This raises another new way of thinking
that we will need to consider.
We celebrate the most profound mysteries of our faith
at Christmas and just before Easter.
These are the most teachable moments we have
in the entire year,
and during these moments we shut our programs down.

We need to begin to think about why we do this.
As long as the shopping mall or school vacation "tail"
continues to wag the dog,
we won't have our faith priorities fully in order.
Profound changes in programming
won't happen overnight.
Don't expect thundering hordes
the first time you stage a morning of reflection
on Holy Saturday morning.
But what better time could there be
for a community of faith
to reflect on the depths of the paschal mystery?
At least give it some thought.

The sample session themes outlined in Chapter 7
are connected to Year A of the lectionary
(except those under the introductory theme "Journey of Faith")
Each theme suggests four topics
that could be offered together in an all-day format
or broken up into a series of shorter time frames.
Each topic follows the same format.
After a brief introduction
and a summary of predictable life connection issues,
the parish explores the topic
employing the following simple, four-part sequence.
Use these sample sessions and the following format
as a guide for your own gatherings.

Seasonal Lectionary Connection
You'll find a reading
chosen from the current year of the lectionary.
This reading guides the core content
of the topic to be examined.
Begin with a proclamation of this reading,
followed by a short period of dialogue.

Use questions similar to those offered
in the Questions of the Week in chapters 4 to 6.
They help participants relate the reading
to their own experience.
It is not important that the reading be
from the last or upcoming Sunday.
The chosen reading will either help recall
an important seasonal reading,
or it will forecast one that is coming up.

Presentation Summary

A synopsis of content for a session presenter
follows the Scripture passages.
This summary reflection touches on important themes
suggested by the *Catechism of the Catholic Church.*
This summary can guide a presentation
of perhaps fifteen to twenty minutes.
Local leaders can add other material
important to the faith needs of their particular parishes.
This scope and sequence could evolve
into a full curriculum for adult faith formation.
If so, a session leader's guide would incorporate
some hands-on processes to accompany the presentation
that would engage the various learning styles
of the participants.

Sample Dialogue Questions

Each presentation summary is followed
by some sample dialogue questions
to guide the faith sharing process.
For intergenerational groupings,
questions for a variety of age groups are suggested.
After a period of reflection suited to local needs,
the session leader would ask for some table feedback,
and draw some conclusions for the group.

Psalm Prayer

Each session closes with a prayer of praise
based on a psalm from the current liturgical season.
A variety of formats could be used to pray the psalm—
men or women reciting alternate verses,
or each table group praying a verse.
Then the leader or other participants
might close with a spontaneous prayer
based on the theme of the psalm.
As you read through the doctrinal themes that follow,
keep in mind the situation of your own parish.
Try to imagine parishioners you know—
children of all ages,
youth at the front and back gates of adolescence,
searching, strong-willed young adults,
hard-working single moms and dads,
couples struggling with jobs and sports programs
and challenging kids,
older adults carrying both wisdom and fear—
all questioning and sharing
and continuing the journey of faith.
They'll laugh and weep
and learn and grow
as they gather in your parish
to share the heritage of faith.

Questions for Discussion

- How has the emergence of new ethnic groups enriched your parish?
- How comfortable are you when others challenge your church's values? How do you respond?
- What benefits do you see to incorporating an intergenerational approach to adult faith formation?
- What obstacles do you see to an intergenerational approach? What could you do to overcome them?

CHAPTER 4

Year A: Questions of the Week

ADVENT THEME: LIGHT OF CHRIST

Note: The theme is the same for all three years. There is also a certain similarity of weekly themes across the three years. Week 1 focuses on watchfulness and taking stock; Week 2, the choice of initiatives for making a deeper response to God's gifts; Week 3, joy at the progress made in doing God's will, followed by increased resolution; and Week 4, submission to God's will as exemplified by Mary and Joseph. Questions for the Feast of the Immaculate Conception can be found in the Seasonal Feasts section at the end of this year.

First Sunday of Advent Putting on the light of Christ

Reading I Isaiah 2:1–5 (Zion, the messianic capital)

Reading II Romans 13:11–14 (Christian use of time)

Gospel Matthew 24:37–44 (the need for watchfulness)

Key Passage Let us then lay aside the works of darkness and put on the armor of light. (Romans 13:12b)

Adult What will you do during Advent so that others can see that you have put on the light of Jesus Christ?

Child What will you do during Advent so that others can see the light of Jesus in you?

Second Sunday of Advent Our need to change

Reading I Isaiah 11:1–10 (the rule of Emmanuel)

Reading II Romans 15:4–9 (prayer of encouragement)

Gospel Matthew 3:1–12 (John the Baptist)

Key Passage This is the one [John the Baptist] of whom the prophet Isaiah spoke when he said, "The voice of one crying out in the wilderness: Prepare the way of the Lord, make his paths straight." (Matthew 3:3)

Adult What do you need to change so that others can learn from watching you that Christ walks among us?

Child What could you do so that others will see in you what it means to follow Jesus?

Third Sunday of Advent Actions worthy of praise

Reading I Isaiah 35:1–6, 10 (Israel's deliverance)

Reading II James 5:7–10 (patience)

Gospel Matthew 11:2–11 (Christ's witness to John)

Key Passage Jesus said, "Truly I tell you, among those born of women no one has arisen greater than John the Baptist; yet the least in the kingdom of heaven is greater than he." (Matthew 11:11)

Adult What would Jesus see to praise about you right now?

Child What good thing have you done so far during Advent to be like Jesus?

Fourth Sunday of Advent Welcoming light

Reading I Isaiah 7:10–14 (birth of Emmanuel)

Reading II Romans 1:1–7 (greetings from Paul)

Gospel Matthew 1:18–24 (the birth of Jesus)

Key Passage When Joseph awoke from sleep, he did as the angel of the Lord commanded him; he took Mary as his wife. (Matthew 1:24)

Adult Whom do you find it difficult to welcome in your life? What can you do to overcome that?

Child What could you do this week to make someone feel welcome, as Joseph welcomed Mary?

CHRISTMASTIME THEME: A SOURCE OF BLESSING

The readings and questions for Christmas can be found in the Seasonal Feasts section at the end of this year.

Holy Family Nurturing family relationships

Reading I Sirach 3:2–6, 12–14 (duties toward parents)

Reading II Colossians 3:12–21 (the practice of virtues)

Gospel Matthew 2:13–15, 19–23 (the flight to Egypt)

Key Passage Joseph got up, took the child and his mother by night, and went to Egypt. (Matthew 2:14)

Adult What can you do this week to help someone in your family feel more secure and loved?

Child What good thing will you do this week to show your love for a parent or grandparent?

Mary, Mother of God Helping others to know God's blessing

Reading I Numbers 6:22–27 (the priestly blessing)

Reading II Galatians 4:4–7 (free sons of God in Christ)

Gospel Luke 2:16–21 (the shepherds' visit, the circumcision)

Key Passage The Lord bless you and keep you; the Lord make his face to shine upon you, and be gracious to you. (Numbers 6:24–25)

Adult How has God blessed and kept your family? What can you do as a family this week to show your gratitude for these blessings?

Child When have you felt most blessed by God? What can you do to help someone in your family feel the same way?

Epiphany A gift for all people

Reading I Isaiah 60:1–6 (glory of the new Zion)

Reading II Ephesians 3:2–3, 5–6 (commission to preach God's plan)

Gospel Matthew 2:1–12 (the visit of the magi)

Key Passage In the time of King Herod, after Jesus was born in Bethlehem of Judea, wise men from the East came to Jerusalem, "Where is the child who has been born king of the Jews? For we observed his star at its rising, and have come to pay him homage." (Matthew 2:1–2)

Adult What insights about your own faith have you gained from learning about other faith traditions?

Child What could you do to be like a star and lead someone to know about Jesus?

Baptism of the Lord Faithful service

Reading I Isaiah 42:1–4, 6–7 (the servant of the Lord)

Reading II Acts 10:34–38 (Peter's discourse)

Gospel Matthew 3:13–17 (the baptism of Jesus)

Key Passage Here is my servant, whom I uphold, my chosen, in whom my soul delights; I have put my spirit upon him; he will bring forth justice to the nations. (Isaiah 42:1)

Adult What evidence can you offer that you are a faithful servant of the Lord?

Child When has the Holy Spirit helped you treat someone fairly?

LENTEN THEME: LIFE THROUGH CHRIST

Questions for Ash Wednesday can be found in the Seasonal Feasts section at the end of this year.

First Sunday of Lent Overcoming temptation

Reading I Genesis 2:7–9; 3:1–7 (the fall of humankind)

Reading II Romans 5:12–19 (humanity's sin through Adam)

Gospel Matthew 4:1–11 (the temptation of Jesus)

Key Passage Jesus was led up by the Spirit into the wilderness to be tempted by the devil. (Matthew 4:1)

Adult What helpful advice could you offer someone faced with a temptation?

Child What helps you do the right thing when you want to do something wrong?

Second Sunday of Lent Call to faithfulness

Reading I Genesis 12:1–4 (call of Abraham)

Reading II 2 Timothy 1:8b–10 (exhortation to faithfulness)

Gospel Matthew 17:1–9 (Jesus transfigured)

Key Passage Six days later, Jesus took with him Peter and James and his brother John and led them up a high mountain, by themselves. And he was transfigured before them, and his face shone like the sun, and his clothes became dazzling white. (Matthew 17:1–2)

Adult How has your faith in Jesus transformed you?

Child How has the example of Jesus helped you become a better person and Christian?

Adult What difference does your faith in Jesus Christ make in your life?

Child What does it mean to you to be a holy person?

Third Sunday of Lent Source of strength

Reading I Exodus 17:3–7 (water from the rock)

Reading II Romans 5:1–2, 5–8 (faith, hope, and love)

Gospel John 4:5–42 (the Samaritan woman at the well)

Key Passage Jesus said to her, "Everyone who drinks of this water will be thirsty again, but those who drink of the water that I will give them will never be thirsty. The water that I will give will become in them a spring of water gushing up to eternal life." (John 4:13–14)

Adult Where have you found a source of "living water" for your own journey of faith?

Child Name some times when your belief in Jesus helped make you stronger.

Fourth Sunday of Lent Source of light

Reading I 1 Samuel 16:1b, 6–7, 10–13a (Samuel anoints David)

Reading II Ephesians 5:8–14 (duty to live in the light)

Gospel John 9:1–41 (the man born blind)

Key Passage For once you were darkness, but now in the Lord you are light. Live as children of light—for the fruit of the light is found in all that is good and right and true. (Ephesians 5:8–9)

Adult What are you doing in your life right now to move toward light rather than darkness?

Child How can you let the light of your faith in Jesus shine for others to see?

Fifth Sunday of Lent Life everlasting

Reading I Ezekiel 37:12–14 (prophecy of restoration)

Reading II Romans 8:8–11 (the flesh and the Spirit)

Gospel John 11:1–45 (the raising of Lazarus)

Key Passage Jesus said to Martha, "I am the resurrection and the life. Those who believe in me, even though they die, will live, and everyone who lives and believes in me will never die. Do you believe this?" (John 11:25–26)

Adult How does belief in the final resurrection from the dead affect your family's daily life?

Child What do you hope for after your life on earth is ended?

Passion (Palm) Sunday Obedience and humility

Procession Gospel Matthew 21:1–11 (triumphal entry into Jerusalem)

Reading I Isaiah 50:4–7 (salvation only through the Lord's servant)

Reading II Philippians 2:6–11 (imitating Christ's humility)

Gospel Matthew 26:14—27:66 (the passion of Jesus)

Key Passage Jesus emptied himself, taking the form of a slave, being born in human likeness. And being found in human form, he humbled himself and became obedient to the point of death—even death on a cross. (Philippians 2:7–8)

Adult How will you try to imitate the obedience and humility of Christ during this holy week?

Child What could you do to show respect for Jesus this week as the church remembers his death and resurrection?

TRIDUUM THEME: THE ETERNAL PASSOVER

Holy Thursday Perfect sacrifice

Reading I Exodus 12:1–8, 11–14 (the Passover ritual prescribed)

Reading II 1 Corinthians 11:23–26 (the Lord's Supper)

Gospel John 13:1–15 (the washing of the feet)

Key Passage For I received from the Lord what I also handed on to you, that the Lord Jesus on the night when he was betrayed took a loaf of bread, and when he had given thanks, he broke it and said, "This is my body that is for you." (1 Corinthians 11:23–24)

Adult What sacrifices did you make out of love?

Child What is the difference between doing something for someone out of love, and doing it because someone makes you?

Good Friday Perfection through suffering

Reading I Isaiah 52:13—53:12 (suffering and triumph of the servant of the Lord)

Reading II Hebrews 4:14–16; 5:7–9 (Jesus, compassionate high priest)

Gospel John 18:1—19:42 (the passion of our Lord Jesus Christ)

Key Passage When you make his life an offering for sin, he shall see his offspring, and shall prolong his days; through him the will of the Lord shall prosper. (Isaiah 53:10)

Adult Can you say that you have grown through your experience of physical or emotional suffering? Why or why not?

Child How can the story of Jesus' suffering make it easier for you to face something painful or uncomfortable?

Holy Saturday (Vigil) New life in Christ

Reading I Genesis 1:1—2:2 (first story of creation)

Reading II Genesis 22:1–18 (the testing of Abraham)

Reading III Exodus 14:15—15:1 (crossing of the Red Sea and destruction of the Egyptians)

Reading IV Isaiah 54:5–14 (the new Zion)

Reading V Isaiah 55:1–11 (an invitation to grace)

Reading VI Baruch 3:9–15, 32—4:4 (prayer of wisdom in the Law of Moses)

Reading VII Ezekiel 36:16–17a, 18–28 (regeneration of the people)

Epistle Romans 6:3–11 (death to sin, life in God)

Gospel Matthew 28:1–10 (the women at the tomb)

Key Passage Therefore we have been buried with him by baptism into death, so that, just as Christ was raised from the dead by the glory of the Father, so we too might walk in newness of life. (Romans 6:4)

Adult What benefits have the new life of baptism brought you so far in your life?

Child If someone who was not a Christian asked you what difference it makes to be baptized, what would you say?

EASTERTIME THEME 1: THE RISEN LORD

Easter Sunday Witness to faith

Reading I Acts 10:34, 37–43 (Peter's discourse)

Reading II Colossians 3:1–4 (mystical death and resurrection)

Or 1 Corinthians 5:6–8 (unleavened bread of sincerity and truth)

Gospel John 20:1–9 (Peter and the disciple at the tomb)

Key Passage Then the other disciple, who reached the tomb first, also went in, and he saw and believed. (John 20:8)

Adult How can you show this week that you truly believe in the resurrection of Jesus?

Child To whom could you tell the story of Jesus' rising from the dead?

Second Sunday of Easter Encouraging others

Reading I Acts 2:42–47 (communal life)

Reading II 1 Peter 1:3–9 (thanksgiving)

Gospel John 20:19–31 (appearance to the disciples; Thomas)

Key Passage Then Jesus said to Thomas, "Put your finger here and see my hands. Reach out your hand and put it in my side. Do not doubt but believe." (John 20:27)

Adult What could you do this week to help strengthen the faith of someone who is faltering?

Child What could you do this week to encourage someone who is sad or discouraged?

Third Sunday of Easter Recognizing the Lord

Reading I Acts 2:14, 22–28 (Peter's discourse)

Reading II 1 Peter 1:17–21 (filial obedience)

Gospel Luke 24:13–35 (Emmaus)

Key Passage When he was at the table with the disciples, he took bread, blessed and broke it, and gave it to them. Then their eyes were opened, and they recognized him; and he vanished from their sight. (Luke 24:30–31)

Adult In what way have you come to know Jesus better through the breaking of the bread at Eucharist?

Child When you join Jesus at the table of the Eucharist next Sunday, what would you like to thank him for?

Fourth Sunday of Easter Called to be shepherds

Reading I Acts 2:14, 36–41 (Peter's discourse)

Reading II 1 Peter 2:20–25 (for the slave)

Gospel John 10:1–10 (the Good Shepherd)

Key Passage [The shepherd] goes ahead of them, and the sheep follow him because they know his voice. (John 10:4)

Adult How are you a shepherd to those in your care?

Child What will you do this week to show you are a Christian?

EASTERTIME THEME 2: THE CALL TO CHRISTIANS

Fifth Sunday of Easter Jesus, the Way

Reading I Acts 6:1–7 (the need of assistants)

Reading II 1 Peter 2:4–9 (living stones)

Gospel John 14:1–12 (last discourse: the way, the truth, and the life)

Key Passage I am the way, and the truth, and the life. No one comes to the Father except through me. (John 14:6)

Adult In a challenge you face right now, what will it mean to live the way of Jesus Christ?

Child Name some ways you can imitate Jesus when you are on the playground or on a sports team.

Sixth Sunday of Easter The strength of faith

Reading I Acts 8:5–8, 14–17 (Philip in Samaria)

Reading II 1 Peter 3:15–18 (on Christian suffering)

Gospel John 14:15–21 (promise of the Paraclete)

Key Passage Jesus said, "And I will ask the Father, and he will give you another Advocate, to be with you forever." (John 14:16)

Adult What difficulties have you overcome because of your belief in the power of the Holy Spirit?

Child Name some times when you need the help of the Holy Spirit.

Seventh Sunday of Easter Sharing Christ's suffering

Reading I Acts 1:12–14 (return to Jerusalem after the ascension)

Reading II 1 Peter 4:13–16 (blessings of persecution)

Gospel John 17:1–11 (completion of Jesus' work)

Key Passage If you are reviled for the name of Christ, you are blessed, because the spirit of glory, which is the Spirit of God, is resting on you. (1Peter 4:14)

Adult If you were to be criticized or insulted because of your Catholic faith, how would you respond?

Child Why are you proud to be a Catholic Christian?

Questions for the Ascension can be found in the Seasonal Feasts section at the end of this year.

Pentecost Sent to serve

Reading I Acts 2:1–11 (descent of the Holy Spirit)

Reading II 1 Corinthians 12:3–7, 12–13 (many gifts, one Spirit, and the analogy of the body)

Gospel John 20:19–23 (appearance to the disciples)

Key Passage Jesus said to them again, "Peace be with you. As the Father has sent me, so I send you." When he had said this, he breathed on them and said to them, "Receive the Holy Spirit." (John 20:21–22)

Adult What important work does Jesus ask of you at this time in your life?

Child How would Jesus want you to treat your friends and family this week?

ORDINARY TIME THEME 1: THE REIGN OF GOD

Trinity Sunday A God of love

Reading I Exodus 34:4–6, 8–9 (renewal of the tablets)

Reading II 2 Corinthians 13:11–13 (farewell)

Gospel John 3:16–18 (belief in the Son sent by the Father)

Key Passage For God so loved the world that he gave his only Son, so that everyone who believes in him may not perish but may have eternal life. (John 3:16)

Adult How could God's mercy and love for the world be revealed through you this week?

Child Do you know anyone who is sick or feeling badly and whom you could visit?

Body and Blood of Christ Bread for others

Reading I Deuteronomy 8:2–3, 14–16 (God's care)

Reading II 1 Corinthians 10:16–17 (the Eucharist vs. pagan sacrifices)

Gospel John 6:51–58 (the living bread)

Key Passage I am the living bread that came down from heaven. Whoever eats of this bread will live forever; and the bread that I will give for the life of the world is my flesh. (John 6:51)

Adult What does it mean for you right now to be bread for others as Jesus was?

Child In what ways can Jesus' presence in the Eucharist help you do good things for others?

Second Sunday in Ordinary Time Jesus, the Son of God

Reading I Isaiah 49:3, 5–6 (the servant of the Lord)

Reading II 1 Corinthians 1:1–3 (greeting to the church)

Gospel John 1:29–34 (John's testimony to Jesus)

Key Passage [John said,] "I myself did not know him; but I came baptizing with water for this reason, that he might be revealed to Israel." (John 1:31)

Adult When have you been surprised to see goodness that you had overlooked in someone?

Child Who has surprised you by doing something kind for you when you did not expect it?

Third Sunday in Ordinary Time Following Jesus

Reading I Isaiah 8:23—9:3 (the Prince of Peace)

Reading II 1 Corinthians 1:10–13, 17 (factions)

Gospel Matthew 4:12–23 (Jesus in Capernaum)

Key Passage Jesus went throughout Galilee, teaching in their synagogues and proclaiming the good news of the kingdom and curing every disease and every sickness among the people. (Matthew 4:23)

Adult To whom could you preach the gospel of Jesus Christ this week with actions rather than words?

Child What could you do for someone this week that would tell them something about Jesus?

Fourth Sunday in Ordinary Time Blessed are we

Reading I Zephaniah 2:3; 3:12–13 (promise for Jerusalem)

Reading II 1 Corinthians 1:26–31 (paradox of God's choice)

Gospel Matthew 5:1–12 (the beatitudes)

Key Passage Blessed are you when people revile you and persecute you and utter all kinds of evil against you falsely on my account. Rejoice and be glad, for your reward is great in heaven, for in the same way they persecuted the prophets who were before you. (Matthew 5:11–12)

Adult Do you believe everyone is welcome in the reign of God? Why or why not?

Child Who is welcome in the reign of God? Who would you like to tell about the reign of God?

Fifth Sunday in Ordinary Time Spreading the light of Christ

Reading I Isaiah 58:7–10 (true fasting)

Reading II 1 Corinthians 2:1–5 (preaching on Christ crucified)

Gospel Matthew 5:13–16 (the similes of salt and light)

Key Passage Jesus said, "In the same way, let your light shine before others, so that they may see your good works and give glory to your Father in heaven." (Matthew 5:16)

Adult In what way might you be hiding the light of Christ from others? What could you do to improve this?

Child How can you let the light of Christ in you shine for others this week?

ORDINARY TIME THEME 2: CHALLENGES TO FAITHFULNESS

Sixth Sunday in Ordinary Time Implications of the new law

Reading I Sirach 15:15–20 (man's free will)

Reading II 1 Corinthians 2:6–10 (true wisdom)

Gospel Matthew 5:17–37 (the old Law and the new)

Key Passage Jesus said, "So when you are offering your gift at the altar, if you remember that your brother or sister has something against you, leave your gift there before the altar and go; first be reconciled to your brother or sister, and then come and offer your gift." (Matthew 5:23–24)

Adult When in your life have you been able to keep the spirit as well as the letter of God's law?

Child When have you taken the first step to make up with someone?

Seventh Sunday in Ordinary Time Love of enemies

Reading I Leviticus 19:1–2, 17–18 (various rules of conduct)

Reading II 1 Corinthians 3:16–23 (the work of God's ministers)

Gospel Matthew 5:38–48 (new law of retaliation; love of enemies)

Key Passage Jesus said, "You have heard that it was said, 'You shall love your neighbor and hate your enemy.' But I say to you, Love your enemies and pray for those who persecute you." (Matthew 5:43–44a)

Adult What is the point of "turning the other cheek" in an argument, and why is it so hard to do?

Child When have you or someone you know insisted on "having the last word" in an argument? What happened afterwards?

Eighth Sunday in Ordinary Time Overcoming fear

Reading I Isaiah 49:14–15 (restoration of Zion)

Reading II 1 Corinthians 4:1–6 (Christ judges his ministers)

Gospel Matthew 6:24–34 (dependence on God)

Key Passage Jesus said, "But if God so clothes the grass of the field, which is alive today and tomorrow is thrown into the oven, will he not much more clothe you—you of little faith?" (Matthew 6:30)

Adult What things do you worry about most frequently? How do you deal with your worry?

Child What can help you worry less about something that might happen?

Ninth Sunday in Ordinary Time Knowing our strength

Reading I Deuteronomy 11:18, 26–28 (reward of fidelity)

Reading II Romans 3:21–25a, 28 (justice apart from the Law)

Gospel Matthew 7:21–27 (conclusion of Sermon on the Mount)

Key Passage Jesus said, "Everyone then who hears these words of mine and acts on them will be like a wise man who built his house on rock. The rain fell, the floods came, and the winds blew and beat on that house, but it did not fall, because it had been founded on rock." (Matthew 7:24–25)

Adult What values have provided a strong foundation for you and your family?

Child What have you learned from your family that helps you make good decisions?

Tenth Sunday in Ordinary Time Lord of mercy

Reading I Hosea 6:3–6 (insincere conversion)

Reading II Romans 4:18–25 (inheritance through faith)

Gospel Matthew 9:9–13 (call of Matthew)

Key Passage As Jesus sat at dinner in the house, many tax collectors and sinners came and were sitting with him and his disciples. (Matthew 9:10)

Adult How does the fact of Jesus' dining with sinners challenge you?

Child Who in your class or neighborhood could you help feel more welcome and accepted?

Eleventh Sunday in Ordinary Time The compassion of Jesus

Reading I Exodus 19:2–6a (requirements of the covenant at Sinai)

Reading II Romans 5:6–11 (sinners saved by Christ)

Gospel Matthew 9:36—10:8 (the compassion of Jesus; mission of the Twelve)

Key Passage Cure the sick, raise the dead, cleanse the lepers, cast out demons. You received without payment; give without payment. (Matthew 10:8)

Adult What responsibility do you have to the less fortunate, and how actively are you meeting it?

Child In what ways can you be generous to others this week?

ORDINARY TIME THEME 3: DAILY FAITH

Twelfth Sunday in Ordinary Time The reassurance of faith

Reading I Jeremiah 20:10–13 (Jeremiah's faith in crisis)

Reading II Romans 5:12–15 (mankind's sin through Adam)

Gospel Matthew 10:26–33 (reassurance to the Twelve)

Key Passage Do not fear those who kill the body but cannot kill the soul. (Matthew 10:28a)

Adult When has your faith in Jesus been most seriously tested?

Child What could you do to encourage someone who is feeling hurt?

Thirteenth Sunday in Ordinary Time Showing Christ to others

Reading I 2 Kings 4:8–11, 14–16 (Elisha and the Shunammite woman)

Reading II Romans 6:3–4, 8–11 (death to sin, life in God)

Gospel Matthew 10:37–42 (conditions and rewards of discipleship)

Key Passage Those who find their life will lose it, and those who lose their life for my sake will find it. (Matthew 10:39)

Adult When have you felt more fully alive by giving of yourself to another?

Child When have you been able to put what someone else needs ahead of what you want for yourself?

Fourteenth Sunday in Ordinary Time Laying down your burdens

Reading I Zechariah 9:9–10 (restoration under the Messiah)

Reading II Romans 8:9, 11–13 (indwelling of the Spirit)

Gospel Matthew 11:25–30 (Jesus and his Father)

Key Passage Jesus said, "Come to me, all you that are weary and are carrying heavy burdens, and I will give you rest. Take my yoke upon you, and learn from me; for I am gentle and humble in heart, and you will find rest for your souls." (Matthew 11:28–29)

Adult When has Jesus refreshed you when you felt burdened by problems?

Child What burden do you need Jesus to help you carry?

Fifteenth Sunday in Ordinary Time Seeds of faith

Reading I Isaiah 55:10–11 (triumph of God's word)

Reading II Romans 8:18–23 (destiny of glory)

Gospel Matthew 13:1–23 (parable of the seed)

Key Passage Jesus said, "Other seeds fell among thorns, and the thorns grew up and choked them. Other seeds fell on good soil and brought forth grain, some a hundredfold, some sixty, some thirty." (Matthew 13:7–8)

Adult How do you provide "good soil" for the faith of others to grow?

Child What are you doing to help the seeds of your faith grow each day?

ORDINARY TIME THEME 4: COURAGEOUS FAITH

Sixteenth Sunday in Ordinary Time Overcoming weakness

Reading I Wisdom 12:13, 16–19 (on God's mercy)

Reading II Romans 8:26–27 (the intercession of the Spirit)

Gospel Matthew 13:24–30 (the parable of the weeds)

Key Passage Likewise the Spirit helps us in our weakness; for we do not know how to pray as we ought, but that very Spirit intercedes with sighs too deep for words. (Romans 8:26)

Adult What weakness can the power of the Spirit help you overcome?

Child When will you need the help of the Holy Spirit this week?

Seventeenth Sunday in Ordinary Time Commitment

Reading I 1 Kings 3:5, 7–12 (wisdom of Solomon)

Reading II Romans 8:28–30 (God's love for all)

Gospel Matthew 13:44–46 (the treasure and the pearl)

Key Passage The kingdom of heaven is like treasure hidden in a field, which someone found and hid; then in his joy he goes and sells all that he has and buys that field. (Matthew 13:44)

Adult What would you be willing to "sell," or do without, in order to achieve your dreams for yourself or your family?

Child What good thing do you want so much that you would give up something else to get it?

Eighteenth Sunday in Ordinary Time Acting with courage

Reading I Isaiah 55:1–3 (invitation to grace)

Reading II Romans 8:35, 37–39 (indomitable love of Christ)

Gospel Matthew 14:13–21 (Jesus feeds five thousand)

Key Passage For I am convinced that neither death, nor life, nor angels, nor rulers, nor things present, nor things to come, nor powers, nor height, nor depth, nor anything else in all creation, will be able to separate us from the love of God in Christ Jesus our Lord. (Romans 8:38–39)

Adult To whom could you bring the assurance of Christ's love this week?

Child Do you remember a time when you felt better because someone acted with love?

Nineteenth Sunday in Ordinary Time Faith in the Lord

Reading I 1 Kings 19:9, 11–13 (Elijah's flight to Horeb)

Reading II Romans 9:1–5 (grief for the Jews; God's free choice)

Gospel Matthew 14:22–33 (Jesus walks on water)

Key Passage Jesus immediately reached out his hand and caught him, saying to him, "You of little faith, why did you doubt?" (Matthew 14:31)

Adult When have you doubted God's loving care for you?

Child What helps you keep trying even when you are afraid?

ORDINARY TIME THEME 5 IN CHRIST'S FOOTSTEPS

Twentieth Sunday in Ordinary Time All are welcome

Reading I Isaiah 56:1, 6–7 (the Lord's house open to all)

Reading II Romans 11:13–15, 29–32 (Israel's final conversion; the triumph of God's mercy)

Gospel Matthew 15:21–28 (faith of the Canaanite woman)

Key Passage For my house shall be called a house of prayer for all peoples. (Isaiah 56:7)

Adult When has the faith of someone from another race or culture enriched your own?

Child What could you do to help someone of another race or culture feel more welcome in your neighborhood?

Twenty–first Sunday in Ordinary Time Representatives of Christ

Reading I Isaiah 22:15, 19–23 (Eliakim chosen by God)

Reading II Romans 11:33–36 (praise of God)

Gospel Matthew 16:13–20 (Peter the rock)

Key Passage He said to them, "But who do you say that I am?" Simon Peter answered, "You are the Messiah, the Son of the living God." (Matthew 16:15–16)

Adult Which church leader has most influenced your personal faith?

Child What has your pastor taught you about Jesus?

Twenty-second Sunday in Ordinary Time Come, follow me

Reading I Jeremiah 20:7–9 (Jeremiah's interior crisis)

Reading II Romans 12:1–2 (sacrifice of body and mind)

Gospel Matthew 16:21–27 (first prophecy of passion and resurrection; doctrine of the cross)

Key Passage Then Jesus told his disciples, "If any want to become my followers, let them deny themselves and take up their cross and follow me." (Matthew 16:24)

Adult What has it meant to you to take up your cross and follow Jesus?

Child When has it been hard to be a follower of Jesus?

Twenty-third Sunday in Ordinary Time Helping others grow

Reading I Ezekiel 33:7–9 (the prophet a watchman)

Reading II Romans 13:8–10 (love fulfills the Law)

Gospel Matthew 18:15–20 (fraternal correction)

Key Passage Jesus said, "If another member of the church sins against you, go and point out the fault when the two of you are alone." (Matthew 18:15)

Adult What have you been able to overcome because others patiently loved you?

Child How can you help another person do the right thing?

ORDINARY TIME THEME 6: THE GOSPEL OF FORGIVENESS

Twenty-fourth Sunday in Ordinary Time Forgiveness and mercy

Reading I Sirach 27:30—28:7 (call to forgiveness and mercy)

Reading II Romans 14:7–9 (to live and die for Christ)

Gospel Matthew 18:21–35 (the merciless official)

Key Passage Then Peter came and said to him, "Lord, if another member of the church sins against me, how often should I forgive? As many as seven times?" Jesus said to him, "Not seven times, but, I tell you, seventy-seven times." (Matthew 18:21–22)

Adult When someone hurts you, are you more inclined to be just or to be merciful?

Child When have you forgiven someone who treated you unfairly?

Twenty-fifth Sunday in Ordinary Time God's generosity

Reading I Isaiah 55:6–9 (seeking the Lord)

Reading II Philippians 1:20–24, 27 (spreading the gospel)

Gospel Matthew 20:1–16 (the laborers in the vineyard)

Key Passage [The landowner] said "Take what belongs to you and go; I choose to give to this last the same as I give to you. Am I not allowed to do what I choose with what belongs to me? Or are you envious because I am generous?" (Matthew 20:14–15)

Adult Which has deepened your faith more—being treated justly or being treated with love and care? Who needs you to treat them with care this week?

Child Think of a time when you were very fair, then think of a time when you were very generous. Which felt better?

Twenty-sixth Sunday in Ordinary Time The challenge to forgive

Reading I Ezekiel 18:25–28 (personal responsibility)

Reading II Philippians 2:1–11 (imitating Christ's humility)

Gospel Matthew 21:28–32 (parable of the two sons)

Key Passage A man had two sons; he went to the first and said, "Son, go and work in the vineyard today." He answered, "I will not"; but later he changed his mind and went. The father went to the second and said the same; and he answered, "I go, sir"; but he did not go. Which of the two did the will of his father? They said, "The first." (Matthew 21:28–31)

Adult When have your actions not measured up to your promises? What was the outcome?

Child Why is it important to follow through on your promises to others?

Twenty-seventh Sunday in Ordinary Time Dealing with injustice

Reading I Isaiah 5:1–7 (the vineyard song)

Reading II Philippians 4:6–9 (joy and peace in Christ)

Gospel Matthew 21:33–43 (parable of the tenants)

Key Passage Jesus said, "Therefore I say to you, the kingdom of God will be taken away from you and given to a people that will produce its fruit." (Matthew 21:43)

Adult What would your reaction be if you found that someone you thought you could trust was taking money from you without your knowledge? How would you handle the situation?

Child What would you do if you found out that a friend had not been loyal to you?

ORDINARY TIME THEME 7: FAITH FOR THE WORLD

Twenty-eighth Sunday in Ordinary Time Living our faith

Reading I Isaiah 25:6–10 (a feast for all peoples)

Reading II Philippians 4:12–14, 19–20 (generosity)

Gospel Matthew 22:1–14 (the wedding banquet)

Key Passage Jesus said, "Many are invited, but few are chosen." (Matthew 22:14)

Adult What will you do this week to show God that you understand the relationship between faith and works?

Child What three things can you do this week to show that you are a follower of Jesus?

Twenty-ninth Sunday in Ordinary Time Social responsibility

Reading I Isaiah 45:1, 4–6 (rewards to Cyrus, king of Persia)

Reading II 1 Thessalonians 1:1–5 (a model for believers)

Gospel Matthew 22:15–21 (paying tax to the emperor)

Key Passage At that [Jesus] said to them "Give therefore to the emperor the things that are the emperor's, and to God the things that are God's." (Matthew 22:21)

Adult How much responsibility do you feel the government should take for meeting the needs of the less fortunate in our society? How willing are you to contribute?

Child Who needs help in your neighborhood or community? What could you and your family do to help?

Thirtieth Sunday in Ordinary Time Love of neighbor

Reading I Exodus 22:20–26 (social laws)

Reading II 1 Thessalonians 1:5–10 (a model for believers)

Gospel Matthew 22:34–40 (the greatest commandment)

Key Passage [Jesus] said to him " 'You shall love the Lord your God with all your heart, and with all your soul, and with all your mind.' This is the greatest and first commandment. And a second is like it: 'You shall love your neighbor as yourself.' " (Matthew 22:37–39)

Adult In a practical sense, what is one thing that would change in your life if you loved your neighbor as yourself?

Child Why is it hard sometimes to love your neighbor? How can you do a better job of following Jesus' commandment?

Thirty-first Sunday in Ordinary Time Sincerity of heart

Reading I Malachi 1:14b—2:2b, 8–10 (punishment for imperfect sacrifices)

Reading II 1 Thessalonians 2:7b–9, 13 (Paul's sincerity)

Gospel Matthew 23:1–12 (hypocrisy of the scribes and Pharisees)

Key Passage Jesus said, "Therefore, do whatever they teach you and follow it; but do not do as they do, for they do not practice what they teach." (Matthew 23:3)

Adult Is there an area of your life in which you sometimes feel like a hypocrite?

Child Would you be willing to do a good work if no one would ever know or praise you for it? Why or why not?

ORDINARY TIME THEME 8: THE SUM OF ONE'S YEARS

Thirty-second Sunday in Ordinary Time Actions and consequences

Reading I Wisdom 6:12–16 (the availability of wisdom to those who seek)

Reading II 1 Thessalonians 4:13–18 (resurrection of the dead)

Gospel Matthew 25:1–13 (parable of the ten virgins)

Key Passage Jesus said, "Keep awake therefore, for you know neither the day nor the hour." (Matthew 25:13)

Adult When have you regretted that you did not look ahead and foresee the consequences of an action?

Child Is there something coming up this week that you could be better prepared for? What might happen if you do not prepare?

Thirty-third Sunday in Ordinary Time Using your gifts

Reading I Proverbs 31:10–13, 19–20, 30–31 (the ideal wife)

Reading II 1 Thessalonians 5:1–6 (the need for preparation)

Gospel Matthew 25:14–30 (parable of the silver pieces)

Key Passage [The servant said,] "Master, you handed over to me five talents; see, I have made five more talents." His master said to him, "Well done, good and trustworthy slave; you have been trustworthy in a few things, I will put you in charge of many things; enter into the joy of your master." (Matthew 25:20b–21)

Adult What gift haven't you developed as you had hoped? What could you still do?

Child What gift has God given you? What do you want to do with it?

Christ the King The final judgment

Reading 1: Ezekiel 34:11–12, 15–17 (parable of the shepherds)

Reading II 1 Corinthians 15:20–26, 28 (Christ, the first fruits)

Gospel Matthew 25:31–46 (the last judgment)

Key Passage [The Son of Man] will answer them, "Truly I tell you, just as you did not do it to one of the least of these, you did not do it to me." (Matthew 25:45)

Adult If you were to be judged today by God, what would be your greatest regret? What is one thing you could do to change that?

Child To which person did you especially try to show Jesus' love and care?

SEASONAL FEASTS: CYCLE A

Immaculate Conception

Reading I Genesis 3:9–15, 20 (the fall)

Reading II Ephesians 1:3–6, 11–12 (the Father's plan for salvation)

Gospel Luke 1:26–38 (announcement of the birth of Jesus)

Key Passage Genesis 3:14 (Adam and Eve banned from the garden)

Adult When did you begin to understand that actions have consequences?

Child When have you owned up to something wrong you have done? What happened when you told the truth?

Christmas: Midnight

Reading I Isaiah 9:3–6 (the Prince of Peace)

Reading II Titus 2:11–14 (transforming of life)

Gospel Luke 2:1–14 (the birth of Jesus)

Key Passage Isaiah 9:5 (a child is born)

Adult When you think of the importance Jesus has in your life, what title of praise would you give him?

Child Why do you think Jesus is called the Prince of Peace?

Ash Wednesday

Reading I Joel 2:12–18 (the day of the Lord)

Reading II 2 Corinthians 5:20—6:2 (ministry of reconciliation)

Gospel Matthew 6:1–6, 16–18 (purity of intention; prayer and fasting)

Key Passage Joel 2:13 (conversion of heart)

Adult What attitude of your heart would you like to change during Lent this year?

Child What does it mean to have a change of heart? What could you change in yourself during Lent this year?

Ascension

Reading I Acts 1:1–11 (Jesus' final instructions and ascension)

Reading II Ephesians 1:17–23 (exaltation of Christ)

Gospel Matthew 28:16–20 (I am with you always)

Key Passage Acts 1:8 (power to proclaim the good news)

Adult With whom have you shared the good news of Jesus in the past month?

Child What good news about Jesus could you share with someone?

Assumption: Vigil

Reading I 1 Chronicles 15:3–4, 15; 16:1–2 (the ark brought to Jerusalem)

Reading II 1 Corinthians 15:54–57 (glorification of the body)

Gospel Luke 11:27–28 (true happiness by keeping the word of God)

Key Passage Luke 11:28 (blessing to those who keep the word of God)

Adult When would it be hardest for you to keep the word of God as Mary did?

Child What can you do to honor Mary, the most blessed of all women?

All Saints

Reading I Revelation 7:2–4, 9–14 (rejoicing of the elect)

Reading II 1 John 3:1–3 (children of God)

Gospel Matthew 5:1–12 (the beatitudes)

Key Passage Revelation 7:10 (salvation comes from the Lamb)

Adult What difference does the gift of salvation make in your life?

Child How can you show your gratitude for the gift of salvation?

CHAPTER 5

Year B: Questions of the Week

ADVENT THEME: FAITHFULNESS

Note: The theme is the same for all three years. There is also a certain similarity of weekly themes across the three years. Week 1 focuses on watchfulness and taking stock; Week 2, the choice of initiatives for making a deeper response to God's gifts; Week 3, joy at the progress made in doing God's will, followed by increased resolution; and Week 4, submission to God's will as exemplified by Mary and Joseph. Questions for the Feast of the Immaculate Conception can be found in the Seasonal Feasts section at the end of this year.

First Sunday of Advent God's faithfulness

Reading I Isaiah 63:16–17, 19, 64:2–7 (prayer for the return of God's favor)

Reading II 1 Corinthians 1:3–9 (thanksgiving)

Gospel Mark 13:33–37 (need for watchfulness)

Key Passage God is faithful; by him you were called into the fellowship of his Son, Jesus Christ our Lord. (1 Corinthians 1:9)

Adult At this time, how faithful do you feel you are being to God's plan for you?

Child What good thing might God be asking you to do right now?

Second Sunday of Advent Patience

Reading I Isaiah 40:1–5, 9–11 (promise of salvation)

Reading II 2 Peter 3:8–14 (Christ will come in judgment)

Gospel Mark 1:1–8 (John the Baptist)

Key Passage The Lord is not slow about his promise, as some think of slowness, but is patient with you, not wanting any to perish but all to come to repentance. (2 Peter 3:9)

Adult With whom could you be more patient this week, as God has been patient with you?

Child Whom can you be more patient with?

Third Sunday of Advent Bringing joy through justice

Reading I Isaiah 61:1–2, 10–11 (the mission to the afflicted)

Reading II 1 Thessalonians 5:16–24 (Christian conduct; blessing)

Gospel John 1:6–8, 19–28 (John as witness to the light)

Key Passage I will greatly rejoice in the Lord, my whole being shall exult in my God; for he has clothed me with the garments of salvation. (Isaiah 61:10)

Adult What work of justice could you do this week to bring someone joy?

Child What could you do for someone this week to make them happy?

Fourth Sunday of Advent Acceptance of God's will

Reading I 2 Samuel 7:1–5, 9–11, 16 (the Lord's promises to David)

Reading II Romans 16:25–27 (doxology)

Gospel Luke 1:26–38 (the annunciation of the Lord)

Key Passage Then Mary said, "Here am I, the servant of the Lord; let it be with me according to your word." Then the angel departed from her. (Luke 1:38)

Adult When have you followed the example of Mary and said, "Let it be done to me as you say?"

Child Is there something hard you need to do this week? What might make it easier?

CHRISTMASTIME THEME: CHOSEN ONES OF GOD

Questions for Christmas Day can be found in the Seasonal Feasts section at the end of this year.

Holy Family Compassion

Reading I Sirach 3:2–6, 12–14 (duties toward parents)

Reading II Colossians 3:12–21 (the practice of virtues; the Christian family)

Gospel Luke 2:22–40 (circumcision of Jesus; presentation in the temple)

Key Passage As God's chosen ones, holy and beloved, clothe yourselves with compassion, kindness, humility, meekness, and patience. (Colossians 3:12)

Adult How do your family members know that you are a compassionate person?

Child What family member needs your compassion and kindness right now?

Mary, Mother of God Blessed by God

Reading I Numbers 6:22–27 (the priestly blessing)

Reading II Galatians 4:4–7 (free sons of God in Christ)

Gospel Luke 2:16–21 (the shepherds' visit)

Key Passage So you are no longer a slave but a child, and if a child then also an heir, through God. (Galatians 4:7)

Adult Which of God's blessings are you most thankful for right now?

Child What does it mean to you to be a child of God?

Epiphany Unexpected gifts

Reading I Isaiah 60:1–6 (glory of the new Zion)

Reading II Ephesians 3:2–3, 5–6 (commission to preach God's plan)

Gospel Matthew 2:1–12 (the visit of the magi)

Key Passage On entering the house, they saw the child with Mary his mother. (Matthew 2:10)

Adult When have you found the presence of Christ in an unexpected place?

Child Where and in whom will you look for Jesus this week?

Baptism of the Lord All are welcome

Reading I Isaiah 42:1–4, 6–7 (the servant of the Lord)

Reading II Acts 10:34–38 (Peter's discourse)

Gospel Mark 1:7–11 (the baptism of Jesus)

Key Passage Then Peter began to speak to them: "I truly understand that God shows no partiality, but in every nation anyone who fears him and does what is right is acceptable to him." (Acts 10:34–35)

Adult To whom have you been guilty of showing partiality? What can you do to correct that?

Child How can you help others feel part of your class's or group's games and activities?

LENTEN THEME: THE CALL TO FAITH

Questions for Ash Wednesday can be found in the Seasonal Feasts section at the end of this year.

First Sunday of Lent A change of heart

Reading I Genesis 9:8–15 (covenant with Noah)

Reading II 1 Peter 3:18–22 (the purpose of Christ's suffering)

Gospel Mark 1:12–15 (Jesus' temptation; the call to conversion)

Key Passage For Christ also suffered for sins once for all, the righteous for the unrighteous, in order to bring you to God. (1 Peter 3:18)

Adult When or how could you step away from your daily responsibilities to renew yourself, so that you can do a better job of following in the footsteps of Jesus?

Child What good habit could you work on during Lent so you could grow closer to God?

Second Sunday of Lent The assurance of faith

Reading I Genesis 22:1–2, 9, 10–13, 15–18 (the testing of Abraham)

Reading II Romans 8:31–34 (God's love for humanity)

Gospel Mark 9:2–10 (Jesus transfigured)

Key Passage Then Peter said to Jesus, "Rabbi, it is good for us to be here; let us make three dwellings, one for you, one for Moses, and one for Elijah." (Mark 9:5)

Adult How deeply do you believe that since God is for you, no one can destroy you?

Child What would you like to ask God to do for you and your family?

Third Sunday of Lent Trust and doubt

Reading I Exodus 20:1–17 (the ten commandments)

Reading II 1 Corinthians 1:22–25 (the wisdom and folly of the cross)

Gospel John 2:13–25 (cleansing of the temple)

Key Passage For Jews demand signs and Greeks desire wisdom, but we proclaim Christ crucified, a stumbling block to Jews and foolishness to Gentiles. (1 Corinthians 1:22–23)

Adult When has the message of the cross seemed absurd to you, and when have you seen its wisdom?

Child What puzzles you in the gospel stories? Which story makes you the most hopeful?

Fourth Sunday of Lent Through the eyes of faith

Reading I 2 Chronicles 36:14–17, 19–23 (dissolution of Judah)

Reading II Ephesians 2:4–10 (generosity of God's plan)

Gospel John 3:14–21 (Jesus' teaching to Nicodemus)

Key Passage Jesus said to Nicodemus, "Indeed, God did not send the Son into the world to condemn the world, but in order that the world might be saved through him." (John 3:17)

Adult Do you see the world as basically evil, or as good? What difference does this make in the way you live?

Child Where do you see goodness in God's world?

Fifth Sunday of Lent The reward of faith

Reading I Jeremiah 31:31–34 (the new covenant)

Reading II Hebrews 5:7–9 (Jesus, compassionate high priest)

Gospel John 12:20–33 (the coming of Jesus' hour)

Key Passage Those who love their life lose it, and those who hate their life in this world will keep it for eternal life. (John 12:25)

Adult When and in what way have you seen life come from death?

Child When have you felt stronger because you sacrificed something for a friend or member of your family?

Passion (Palm) Sunday Surrender to God's will

Procession Mark 11:1–10 (entry into Jerusalem) or John 12:12–16

Reading I Isaiah 50:4–7 (salvation only through the Lord's servant)

Reading II Philippians 2:6–11 (imitating Christ's humility)

Gospel Mark 14:1—15:47 (the passion of Jesus)

Key Passage Jesus said, "Abba, Father, for you all things are possible; remove this cup from me; yet, not what I want, but what you want." (Mark 14:36)

Adult When have you found it hardest to accept God's will? What enabled you to accept it?

Child When is it hardest for you to obey?

TRIDUUM THEME: THE LORD'S SUPPER

Holy Thursday Remembrance

Reading I Exodus 12:1–8, 11–14 (the Passover ritual prescribed)

Reading II 1 Corinthians 11:23–26 (the Lord's Supper)

Gospel John 13:1–15 (the washing of the feet)

Key Passage For as often as you eat this bread and drink the cup, you proclaim the Lord's death until he comes. (1Corinthians 11:26)

Adult How has your understanding of the Eucharist increased since you were a child?

Child How does the Mass help you remember the events of Jesus' life and death?

Good Friday The suffering servant

Reading I Isaiah 52:13—53:12 (suffering and triumph of the servant of the Lord)

Reading II Hebrews 4:14–16; 5:7–9 (Jesus, compassionate high priest)

Gospel John 18:1—19:42 (the passion of Jesus)

Key Passage Jesus said to Peter, "Put your sword back into its sheath. Am I not to drink the cup that the Father has given me?" (John 18:11)

Adult What new insight for your life are you receiving through your reflection on the mysteries of Christ's passion during the Holy Week liturgies?

Child What do you think of as you hear the story of Jesus' passion and death?

Holy Saturday From death to life

Reading I Genesis 1:1—2:2 (first story of creation)

Reading II Genesis 22:1–18 (the testing of Abraham)

Reading III Exodus 14:15—15:1 (crossing of the Red Sea and destruction of the Egyptians)

Reading IV Isaiah 54:5–14 (the new Zion)

Reading V Isaiah 55:1–11 (an invitation to grace)

Reading VI Baruch 3:9–15, 32—4:4 (prayer of wisdom in the Law of Moses)

Reading VII Ezekiel 36:16–17a, 18–28 (regeneration of the people)

Epistle Romans 6:3–11 (death to sin, life in God)

Gospel Mark 16:1–8 (the women at the tomb)

Key Passage Seek the Lord while he may be found, call upon him while he is near. (Isaiah 55:6)

Adult How has your celebration of the Eucharist over the years deepened your understanding of life?

Child What have you learned about being a good Christian from your celebration of Sunday Mass?

EASTERTIME THEME 1: EASTER PEOPLE

Easter Sunday Hope of salvation

Reading I Acts 10:34, 37–43 (Peter's discourse)

Reading II Colossians 3:1–4 (mystical death and resurrection) Or 1 Corinthians 5:6–8 (unleavened bread of sincerity and truth)

Gospel John 20:1–9 (Peter and the disciple at the tomb)

Key Passage When Christ who is your life is revealed, then you also will be revealed with him in glory. (Colossians 3:4)

Adult Why do you believe that you will live with Christ for all eternity?

Child Who has helped you believe that you will live with Jesus forever?

Second Sunday of Easter Following the example of Jesus

Reading I Acts 4:32–35 (life of the Christians)

Reading II 1 John 5:1–6 (belief in Jesus Christ)

Gospel John 20:19–31 (appearance to the disciples)

Key Passage Now the whole group of those who believed were of one heart and soul; no one claimed private ownership of any possessions; everything they owned was held in common. (Acts 4:32)

Adult What could you do this week to inspire your family to resemble the early Christians more closely?

Child What could you and your family do to help others who are in need?

Third Sunday of Easter The living Christ

Reading I Acts 3:13–15, 17–19 (Peter's discourse on Jesus' resurrection)

Reading II 1 John 2:1–5 (keeping the commandments)

Gospel Luke 24:35–48 (Jesus appears to the Eleven)

Key Passage Jesus said to them, "Why are you frightened, and why do doubts arise in your hearts? Look at my hands and my feet; see that it is I myself." (Luke 24:38–39)

Adult What questions about Jesus still arise in the midst of your faith?

Child What question would you like to ask someone about Jesus' appearance to the Apostles?

Fourth Sunday of Easter Called to be shepherds

Reading I Acts 4:8–12 (the stone that has become the cornerstone)

Reading II 1 John 3:1–2 (recognizing the Son)

Gospel John 10:11–18 (the Good Shepherd)

Key Passage Jesus said, "I am the good shepherd. The good shepherd lays down his life for the sheep." (John 10:11)

Adult Whom are you shepherding in your life right now, and who shepherds you?

Child Who has been like a shepherd to you by their example? For whom could you be a shepherd?

EASTERTIME THEME 2: A DISCIPLE'S WORK

Fifth Sunday of Easter Strengthening your faith

Reading I Acts 9:26–31 (Saul visits Jerusalem)

Reading II 1 John 3:18–24 (the actions of believers)

Gospel John 15:1–8 (the vine and the branches)

Key Passage [The vine grower] removes every branch in me that bears no fruit. Every branch that bears fruit he prunes to make it bear more fruit. (John 15:2)

Adult When have you been "pruned" by your experiences in a way that led to greater abundance?

Child When have you felt stronger or better because you did something hard to help another person?

Sixth Sunday of Easter Love of your neighbor

Reading I Acts 10:25–26, 34–35, 44–48 (Peter in Caesarea)

Reading II 1 John 4:7–10 (God's love and ours)

Gospel John 15:9–17 (a disciple's love)

Key Passage Jesus said, "This is my commandment, that you love one another as I have loved you." (John 15:12)

Adult How is love of others connected to love for God?

Child Who needs Jesus' love this week? How can you show them his love?

Seventh Sunday of Easter Praying for others

Reading I Acts 1:15–17, 20–26 (Matthias chosen)

Reading II 1 John 4:11–16 (love for one another)

Gospel John 17:11–19 (Jesus' prayer for the disciples)

Key Passage [Jesus prayed to his Father,] "I am asking on their behalf; I am not asking on behalf of the world, but on behalf of those whom you gave me, because they are yours." (John 17:9)

Adult Who needs you to pray for them this week, as Jesus prayed for his disciples?

Child Who will you pray for this week?

Pentecost Acting with courage

Reading I Acts 2:1–11 (descent of the Holy Spirit)

Reading II 1 Corinthians 12:3–7, 12–13 (many gifts, one Spirit, and the analogy of the body)

Gospel John 20:19–23 (appearance to the disciples)

Key Passage Divided tongues, as of fire, appeared among them, and a tongue rested on each of them. All of them were filled with the Holy Spirit and began to speak in other languages, as the Spirit gave them ability. (Acts 2:3–4)

Adult When has the Holy Spirit given you the strength to act with courage?

Child When and where do you need the Holy Spirit's help to speak out?

ORDINARY TIME THEME 1: SIGNS OF GOD'S PRESENCE

Trinity Sunday Signs of God's love

Reading I Deuteronomy 4:32–34, 39–40 (proofs of God's love)

Reading II Romans 8:14–17 (sons of God through adoption)

Gospel Matthew 28:16–20 (commission of the Apostles)

Key Passage Moses said to the people, "For ask now about former ages, long before your own, ever since the day that God created human beings on the earth; ask from one end of heaven to the other: has anything so great as this ever happened or has its like ever been heard of?" (Deuteronomy 4:32)

Adult What signs of God's love have you witnessed in your life?

Child How can you be a sign of God's love to others this week?

Body and Blood of Christ Bread for others

Reading I Exodus 24:3–8 (ratification of the covenant)

Reading II Hebrews 9:11–15 (the sacrifice of Jesus)

Gospel Mark 14:12–16, 22–26 (Passover preparation)

Key Passage While they were eating, he took a loaf of bread, and after blessing it he broke it, gave it to them, and said, "Take; this is my body." (Mark 14:22)

Adult In what ways have you practiced the words of Jesus and been bread for others?

Child What can you do to prepare to celebrate Holy Communion with your parish family?

ORDINARY TIME THEME 2: DISCIPLESHIP

Second Sunday in Ordinary Time Come and see

Reading I 1 Samuel 3:3–10, 19 (revelation to Samuel)

Reading II 1 Corinthians 6:13–15, 17–20 (against sexual immorality)

Gospel John 1:35–42 (the first disciples)

Key Passage They said to him, "Rabbi" (which translated means Teacher), "where are you staying?" He said to them, "Come and see." They came and saw where he was staying, and they remained with him that day. (John 1:38b–39)

Adult What qualities do you have that would cause others to recognize you as a disciple of Jesus?

Child What does it take to be a follower of Jesus?

Third Sunday in Ordinary Time Repent and believe

Reading I Jonah 3:1–5, 10 (conversion of Nineveh)

Reading II 1 Corinthians 7:29–31 (encouragement within a hostile world)

Gospel Mark 1:14–20 (call of the first disciples)

Key Passage Now after John was arrested, Jesus came to Galilee, proclaiming the good news of God, and saying, "The time is fulfilled, and the kingdom of God has come near; repent, and believe in the good news." (Mark 1:14–15)

Adult What part of your life is Jesus calling you to change right now?

Child In what way do you think you can be a better follower of Jesus?

Fourth Sunday in Ordinary Time Sharing good news

Reading I Deuteronomy 18:15–20 (a prophet like Moses)

Reading II 1 Corinthians 7:32–35 (the state of virginity)

Gospel Mark 1:21–28 (cure of a demoniac)

Key Passage They were astounded at his teaching, for he taught them as one having authority, and not as the scribes. (Mark 1:22)

Adult What can you tell others about Jesus with the most assurance?

Child What is the most important thing you would like others to know about Jesus? How will you show or tell them?

Fifth Sunday in Ordinary Time Comfort for the sorrowful

Reading I Job 7:1–4, 6–7 (Job's first reply)

Reading II 1 Corinthians 9:16–19, 22–23 (Paul's recompense)

Gospel Mark 1:29–39 (cure of Peter's mother-in-law and other miracles)

Key Passage That evening, at sundown, they brought to him all who were sick or possessed with demons. And the whole city was gathered around the door. And he cured many who were sick with various diseases, and cast out many demons. (Mark 1:32–34a)

Adult When have you felt the sadness of Job? When have you felt the joy of those who witnessed the healing works of Jesus?

Child What could you do this week to comfort someone who is sad?

ORDINARY TIME THEME 3: IMITATING CHRIST

Sixth Sunday in Ordinary Time Models of Christ

Reading I Leviticus 13:1–2, 44–46 (on leprosy)

Reading II 1 Corinthians 10:31—11:1 (imitation of Christ)

Gospel Mark 1:40–45 (healing of a leper)

Key Passage Be imitators of me, as I am of Christ. (1 Corinthians 11:1)

Adult Would you have the courage to tell others to do as you do in order to be a Christian? Why or why not?

Child What can you do this week to be an example to others?

Seventh Sunday in Ordinary Time The test of faith

Reading I Isaiah 43:18–19, 21,22, 24b–25 (promise of redemption and restoration)

Reading II 2 Corinthians 1:18–22 (Paul's sincerity)

Gospel Mark 2:1–12 (healing of a paralytic at Capernaum)

Key Passage Jesus said, "Which is easier, to say to the paralytic, 'Your sins are forgiven,' or to say, 'Stand up and take your mat and walk'?" (Mark 2:9)

Adult When has it been hardest for you to believe that your sins are forgiven?

Child Are you willing to believe what you cannot see? Why is this hard to do?

Eighth Sunday in Ordinary Time Witnesses of faith

Reading I Hosea 2:18b, 17b, 21–22 (Israel's restoration)

Reading II 2 Corinthians 3:1b–6 (ministers of the new covenant)

Gospel Mark 2:18–22 (the question of fasting)

Key Passage You yourselves are our letter, written on our hearts, to be known and read by all. (2 Corinthians 3:2)

Adult If you thought of your life as a letter of faith, what would it say?

Child If someone were to write a letter about you and your faith, what would they say?

Ninth Sunday in Ordinary Time Worshiping God

Reading I Deuteronomy 5:12–15 (the Decalogue: the Sabbath)

Reading II 2 Corinthians 4:6–11 (treasure in earthen vessels)

Gospel Mark 2:23—3:6 (the disciples and the Sabbath)

Key Passage The Son of Man is lord even of the sabbath. (Mark 2:28)

Adult How do you witness to others that you and your family believe Sunday is a holy day?

Child What do you and your family do to honor God on Sunday?

Tenth Sunday in Ordinary Time Love for all

Reading I Genesis 3:9–15 (the fall)

Reading II 2 Corinthians 4:13–5:1 (paradox of the ministry)

Gospel Mark 3:20–35 (Jesus and Beelzebul; Jesus and his family)

Key Passage Jesus said, "Whoever does the will of God is my brother and sister and mother." (Mark 3:35)

Adult In what way could you widen the circle of your family to include someone in need?

Child Whom could you invite to share a happy time with your family?

Eleventh Sunday in Ordinary Time Living in God's kingdom

Reading I Ezekiel 17:22–24 (prophecy of the restoration of Israel)

Reading II 2 Corinthians 5:6–10 (walking by faith)

Gospel Mark 4:26–34 (seed grows by itself and the mustard seed)

Key Passage Yet when [the mustard seed] is sown it grows up and becomes the greatest of all shrubs, and puts forth large branches, so that the birds of the air can make nests in its shade. (Mark 4:32)

Adult What is the "good soil" that has allowed your faith to grow like the mustard seed and provide shelter for others?

Child How do you help your faith grow like the mustard seed?

Twelfth Sunday in Ordinary Time Gift of peace

Reading I Job 38:1, 8–11 (the Lord's speech to Job)

Reading II 2 Corinthians 5:14–17 (the ministry of reconciliation)

Gospel Mark 4:35–41 (the storm on the sea)

Key Passage Jesus said to the sea, "Peace! Be still!" Then the wind ceased, and there was a dead calm. He said to them, "Why are you afraid? Have you still no faith?" (Mark 4:39–40)

Adult When has the Lord calmed the stormy seas of your life?

Child What fear would you like the Lord to help you overcome?

ORDINARY TIME THEME 4: QUALITIES OF DISCIPLES

Thirteenth Sunday in Ordinary Time Rich in love

Reading I Wisdom 1:13–15; 2:23–24 (God's justice and its rejection by the wicked)

Reading II 2 Corinthians 8:7, 9:13–15 (liberal giving)

Gospel Mark 5:21–43 (the daughter of Jairus; the woman with a hemorrhage)

Key Passage For you know the generous act of our Lord Jesus Christ, that though he was rich, yet for your sakes he became poor, so that by his poverty you might become rich. (2 Corinthians 8:9)

Adult When have you felt enriched by a sacrifice you made for another?

Child Whom could you help by your acts of kindness this week?

Fourteenth Sunday in Ordinary Time Self-acceptance

Reading I Ezekiel 2:2–5 (the Lord speaks to Ezekiel)

Reading II 2 Corinthians 12:7–10 (Paul's weakness)

Gospel Mark 6:1–6 (Jesus at Nazareth)

Key Passage [Paul said,] Three times I appealed to the Lord about this, that it would leave me, but he said to me, "My grace is sufficient for you, for power is made perfect in weakness." (2 Corinthians 12:8)

Adult What unavoidable weakness in yourself do you struggle to accept?

Child What have you wished would be different or better about you?

Fifteenth Sunday in Ordinary Time Sharing good news

Reading I Amos 7:12–15 (Amos called by God to prophesy)

Reading II Ephesians 1:3–14 (blessing for Jew and Gentile)

Gospel Mark 6:7–13 (the mission of the Twelve)

Key Passage He called the twelve and began to send them out two by two, and gave them authority over the unclean spirits. (Mark 6:7)

Adult What good news of Jesus can you share with others this week?

Child What good news of Jesus can you share with others this week?

Sixteenth Sunday in Ordinary Time Come away and rest

Reading I Jeremiah 23:1–6 (messianic reign)

Reading II Ephesians 2:13–18 (all united in Christ)

Gospel Mark 6:30–34 (return of the disciples)

Key Passage The apostles gathered around Jesus, and told him all that they had done and taught. He said to them, "Come away to a deserted place all by yourselves and rest a while." (Mark 6:30–31a)

Adult What do you do to rest so that you can return to work refreshed?

Child When will you take time to stop and pray this week?

ORDINARY TIME THEME 5: BREAD OF LIFE

Seventeenth Sunday in Ordinary Time Gifts of hope

Reading I 2 Kings 4:42–44 (Elisha: the multiplication of loaves)

Reading II Ephesians 4:1–6 (unity in the Mystical Body)

Gospel John 6:1–15 (multiplication of the loaves)

Key Passage When [the people] were satisfied, he told his disciples, "Gather up the fragments left over, so that nothing may be lost." So they gathered them up, and from the fragments of the five barley loaves, left by those who had eaten, they filled twelve baskets. (John 6:12–13)

Adult When has the generous gift of another offered you hope?

Child What loving gift could you give to another person this week?

Eighteenth Sunday in Ordinary Time The eyes of faith

Reading I Exodus 16:2–4, 12–15 (manna in the desert)

Reading II Ephesians 4:17, 20–24 (renewal in Christ)

Gospel John 6:24–28 (discourse on the bread of life)

Key Passage So they said to Jesus, "What sign are you going to give us then, so that we may see it and believe you? What work are you performing?" (John 6:30)

Adult When has your faith helped you believe without "seeing signs" from God?

Child Who helps you believe in things you cannot see?

Nineteenth Sunday in Ordinary Time Life for the world

Reading I 1 Kings 19:4–8 (Elijah's flight to Horeb)

Reading II Ephesians 4:30—5:2 (vices to be avoided)

Gospel John 6:41–51 (discourse on the bread of life, continued)

Key Passage Jesus said, "I am the living bread that came down from heaven. Whoever eats of this bread will live forever; and the bread that I will give for the life of the world is my flesh." (John 6:51)

Adult When has the bread of life given you the strength you needed to face a difficult situation in your life?

Child What will you ask Jesus to help you with when you receive Holy Communion this week?

Twentieth Sunday in Ordinary Time Promise of eternal life

Reading I Proverbs 9:1–6 (forsake foolishness)

Reading II Ephesians 5:15–20 (sing praise to the Lord)

Gospel John 6:51–58 (discourse on the bread of life, continued)

Key Passage Jesus said, "Those who eat my flesh and drink my blood have eternal life, and I will raise them up on the last day." (John 6:54)

Adult How does Jesus' promise of eternal life affect the way you live today?

Child How often do you think about heaven? Does it make a difference in the choices you make?

ORDINARY TIME THEME 6: RESPONDING TO GOD'S GIFTS

Twenty-first Sunday in Ordinary Time Christian marriage

Reading I Joshua 24:1–2, 15–17, 18 (reminder of the divine goodness)

Reading II Ephesians 5:21–32 (Christian wives and husbands)

Gospel John 6:60–69 (effect of the bread of life discourse)

Key Passage This is a great mystery, and I am applying it to Christ and the church. Each of you, however, should love his wife as himself, and a wife should respect her husband. (Ephesians 5:32–33)

Adult In what way has the example of Christian marriage (your own or that of another couple) helped you understand the relationship between Christ and his church?

Child What can you do for your family to show them Jesus' love and care?

Twenty-second Sunday in Ordinary Time Doers of the word

Reading I Deuteronomy 4:1–2, 6–8 (advantages of fidelity)

Reading II James 1:17–18, 21–22, 27 (response to God's gift)

Gospel Mark 7:1–8, 14–15, 21–23 (Jesus and the Pharisees)

Key Passage Welcome with meekness the implanted word that has the power to save your souls. But be doers of the word, and not merely hearers who deceive themselves. (James 1:21–22)

Adult Which words of Jesus provide the most inspiration for the Christian work that you do?

Child How do you welcome the words of Jesus into your heart?

Twenty-third Sunday in Ordinary Time Rich in faith

Reading I Isaiah 35:4–7 (Israel's deliverance)

Reading II James 2:1–5 (against favoritism)

Gospel Mark 7:31–37 (healing of a deaf-mute)

Key Passage Listen, my beloved brothers and sisters. Has not God chosen the poor in the world to be rich in faith and to be heirs of the kingdom that he has promised to those who love him? (James 2:5)

Adult When has your faith in Jesus enabled you to speak out on an issue of importance?

Child What does your belief in Jesus mean to you?

Twenty-fourth Sunday in Ordinary Time Faith and works

Reading I Isaiah 50:4–9 (salvation through the Lord's servant)

Reading II James 2:14–18 (faith and good works)

Gospel Mark 8:27–35 (first teaching of the paschal event and the doctrine of the cross)

Key Passage Faith by itself, if it has no works, is dead. But someone will say, "You have faith and I have works." Show me your faith apart from your works, and I by my works will show you my faith. (James 2:17–18)

Adult Why should faith always lead to good works?

Child What good works can you do to show your faith in Jesus?

ORDINARY TIME THEME 7: GODLY POWER

Twenty-fifth Sunday in Ordinary Time True wisdom

Reading I Wisdom 2:1, 17–20 (the wicked speak)

Reading II James 3:16—4:3 (true wisdom and worldly desires)

Gospel Mark 9:30–37 (second teaching of the paschal event and words against ambition and envy)

Key Passage He sat down, called the twelve, and said to them, "Whoever wants to be first must be last of all and servant of all." (Mark 9:35)

Adult What evidence do you see in the world around you that many do not accept Jesus' teaching on power and ambition?

Child Why is it wrong to feel envy for what belongs to another?

Twenty-sixth Sunday in Ordinary Time Setting priorities

Reading I Numbers 11:25–29 (sharing the gift of prophecy)

Reading II James 5:1–6 (saving the right focus)

Gospel Mark 9:38–43, 45, 47–48 (sharing our possessions)

Key Passage Listen! The wages of the laborers who mowed your fields, which you kept back by fraud, cry out, and the cries of the harvesters have reached the ears of the Lord of hosts. (James 5:4)

Adult What are the three most important values motivating your daily decisions?

Child Could a poor person who is wise be richer in a way than a foolish person who has many things? Why?

Twenty-seventh Sunday in Ordinary Time Childlike faith

Reading I Genesis 2:18–24 (second story of creation, the creation of woman)

Reading II Hebrew 2:9–11 (Jesus' exaltation through abasement)

Gospel Mark 10:2–16 (question of divorce and Jesus blessing the children)

Key Passage Jesus said, "Truly I tell you, whoever does not receive the kingdom of God as a little child will never enter it." (Mark 10:15)

Adult What could keep you from embracing the kingdom of God like a little child?

Child How do you feel when you hear the wonderful stories of God's love for you?

Twenty-eighth Sunday in Ordinary Time Danger of riches

Reading I Wisdom 7:7–11 (Solomon and the riches of wisdom)

Reading II Hebrews 4:12–13 (God's living word)

Gospel Mark 10:17–30 or 10:17–27 (the danger of riches—Jesus and the rich man)

Key Passage Jesus said, "It is easier for a camel to go through the eye of a needle than for someone who is rich to enter the kingdom of God." (Mark 10:25)

Adult How can the pleasures and comforts of this world become barriers to your relationship with God?

Child What favorite toy, game, video, etc., of yours would you be willing to share with someone this week?

Twenty-ninth Sunday in Ordinary Time Quiet sacrifice

Reading I Isaiah 53:10–11 (the suffering servant)

Reading II Hebrews 4:14–16 (Jesus, compassionate high priest)

Gospel Mark 10:35–45 (ambition of James and John)

Key Passage Jesus said, "Whoever wishes to become great among you must be your servant, and whoever wishes to be first among you must be slave of all." (Mark 10:44)

Adult Why is it hard to do good works if you will not be acknowledged for them?

Child Are you willing to do a good deed even if no one knows that you did it? Why?

ORDINARY TIME THEME 8: THE REWARDS OF FAITH

Thirtieth Sunday in Ordinary Time The eyes of faith

Reading I Jeremiah 31:7–9 (the restoration)

Reading II Hebrews 5:1–6 (Jesus, the high priest)

Gospel Mark 10:46–52 (the blind Bartimaeus)

Key Passage Jesus said to him, "Go; your faith has made you well." Immediately he regained his sight and followed him on the way. (Mark 10:52)

Adult What have your eyes of faith helped you see in a new way?

Child What do you like most about the story of Bartimaeus? Why?

Thirty-first Sunday in Ordinary Time The greatest commandment

Reading I Deuteronomy 6:2–6 (the great commandment)

Reading II Hebrews 7:23–28 (Jesus, the eternal high priest)

Gospel Mark 12:28–34 (the greatest commandment)

Key Passage [The scribe] asked him, "Which commandment is the first of all?" Jesus answered, "The first is, 'Hear, O Israel: the Lord our God, the Lord is one; you shall love the Lord your God with all your heart, and with all your soul, and with all your mind, and with all your strength.'" (Mark 12:28–30)

Adult Why is love of neighbor as important as love of God?

Child When do you show that you love God and your neighbor with your whole heart?

Thirty-second Sunday in Ordinary Time Giving from our need

Reading I 1 Kings 17:10–16 (Elijah and the widow)

Reading II Hebrews 9:24–28 (the sacrifice of Jesus)

Gospel Mark 12:38–44 (hypocrisy of the scribes, and the widow's mite)

Key Passage Jesus said, "Truly I tell you, this poor widow has put in more than all those who are contributing to the treasury. For all of them have contributed out of their abundance; but she out of her poverty has put in everything she had, all she had to live on." (Mark 12:43–44)

Adult What are you willing to give out of love for God that would be a hardship for you?

Child What would you be willing to give up for someone else?

Thirty-third Sunday in Ordinary Time Ready for the Lord

Reading I Daniel 12:1–3 (Daniel's conclusion to the apocalypse)

Reading II Hebrews 10:11–14, 18 (Christ's eternal sacrifice)

Gospel Mark 13:24–32 (the second coming)

Key Passage Jesus said, "Beware, keep alert; for you do not know when the time will come." (Mark 13:33)

Adult What would you be doing differently in your life if you truly believed you would meet Christ soon?

Child What would you do for others today if you thought you would not have another chance to do it?

Christ the King Given the kingdom

Reading I Daniel 7:13–14 (Daniel's vision of one like the Son of man)

Reading II Revelation 1:5–8 (praise to Jesus Christ)

Gospel John 18:33–37 (the blood and water)

Key Passage To him who loves us and freed us from our sins by his blood, and made us to be a kingdom, priests serving his God and Father, to him be glory and dominion forever and ever. Amen. (Revelation: 1:5b–6)

Adult In what ways is Jesus the ruler of your life?

Child How can you show that you honor Jesus as the king of your life?

SEASONAL FEASTS: CYCLE B

Immaculate Conception

Reading I Genesis 3:9–15, 20 (the fall)

Reading II Ephesians 1:3–6, 11–12 (the Father's plan for salvation)

Gospel Luke 1:26–38 (announcement of the birth of Jesus)

Key Passage Luke 1:38 (Mary consents to the angel's announcement)

Adult When has it been hard to say yes to God when faced with a difficult challenge?

Child What blessings has God given to you and your family?

Christmas: Dawn

Reading I Isaiah 62:11–12 (your salvation comes)

Reading II Titus 3:4–7 (the loving kindness of God our Savior appeared)

Gospel Luke 2:15–20 (the birth of the Savior)

Key Passage Luke 2:19 (Mary treasures these events in her heart)

Adult What will you do during this Christmas season to reflect in your heart, as Mary did, on God's gift of the Savior?

Child What would you say to Jesus as you stand before the nativity scene in your church?

Ash Wednesday

Reading I Joel 2:12–18 (the day of the Lord)

Reading II 2 Corinthians 5:20—6:2 (ministry of reconciliation)

Gospel Matthew 6:1–6, 16–18 (purity of intention; prayer and fasting)

Key Passage Matthew 6:1 (expect no public praise for good works)

Adult What good work could you do this week without seeking acknowledgment or praise from others?

Child What good work could you do this week without telling others that you have done it?

Ascension

Reading I Acts 1:1–11 (Jesus' final instructions and ascension)

Reading II Ephesians 1:17–23 (exaltation of Christ)

Gospel Mark 16:15–20 (conclusion of Mark's gospel)

Key Passage Mark 16:15 (go and proclaim the good news)

Adult How well are you fulfilling Jesus' command to share the good news with others?

Child Why are Christians filled with hope?

Assumption: Day

Reading I Revelation 11:19; 12:1–6, 10 (the woman and the dragon)

Reading II 1 Corinthians 15:20–26 (Christ, the first fruits)

Gospel Luke 1:39–56 (Mary's visit to Elizabeth)

Key Passage Luke 1:49 ("God has done great things for me")

Adult What do you trust that God will do for you?

Child What gift of God makes you happy and joyful?

All Saints

Reading I Revelation 7:2–4, 9–14 (rejoicing of the elect)

Reading II 1 John 3:1–3 (children of God)

Gospel Matthew 5:1–12 (the beatitudes)

Key Passage Matthew 5:12 (blest are you)

Adult What is the greatest challenge of the beatitudes for you?

Child What does it mean to be blessed by God?

CHAPTER 6

Year C: Questions of the Week

ADVENT THEME: CALL TO HOLINESS

Note: The theme is the same for all three years. There is also a certain similarity of weekly themes across the three years. Week 1 focuses on watchfulness and taking stock; Week 2, the choice of initiatives for making a deeper response to God's gifts; Week 3, joy at the progress made in doing God's will, followed by increased resolution; and Week 4, submission to God's will as exemplified by Mary and Joseph. Questions for the Feast of the Immaculate Conception are in the Seasonal Feasts section at the end of this year.

First Sunday of Advent The habit of prayer

Reading I Jeremiah 33:14–16 (restoration of Jerusalem)

Reading II 1 Thessalonians 3:12—4:2 (plea for growth in holiness)

Gospel Luke 21:25–28, 34–36 (coming of the Son of Man)

Key Passage Be alert at all times, praying that you may have the strength to escape all these things that will take place, and to stand before the Son of Man. (Luke 21:36)

Adult What have been the strengths of your prayer life? What habit of prayer could you strengthen during this Advent season?

Child What prayers will you say each day and each week during Advent?

Second Sunday of Advent Prayer of repentance

Reading I Baruch 5:1–9 (Jerusalem consoled)

Reading II Philippians 1:4–6, 8–11 (gratitude and hope)

Gospel Luke 3:1–6 (John the Baptist)

Key Passage John went into all the region around the Jordan, proclaiming a baptism of repentance for the forgiveness of sins. (Luke 3:3)

Adult In what areas of your life do you need God's forgiveness right now? What Advent practice would assist you in expressing your repentance?

Child What do you want to ask God to forgive you for? What can you do during Advent to show you are sorry?

Third Sunday of Advent The joy of kindness

Reading I Zephaniah 3:14–18a (promise of a Savior)

Reading II Philippians 4:4–7 (joy and peace)

Gospel Luke 3:10–18 (John calls the people to justice)

Key Passage Rejoice in the Lord always; again I will say, Rejoice. Let your gentleness be known to everyone. (Philippians 4:4–5)

Adult To whom have your past acts of kindness brought joy? What act of kindness could you do this week?

Child What kind thing have you done for someone lately? Whom could you make happy by your kindness this week?

Fourth Sunday of Advent Obedience to God's will

Reading I Micah 5:1–4a (restoration through the Messiah)

Reading II Hebrews 10:5–10 (the second covenant)

Gospel Luke 1:39–45 (the visit to Elizabeth)

Key Passage Elizabeth said, "Blessed is she who believed that there would be a fulfillment of what was spoken to her by the Lord." (Luke 1:45)

Adult When was it hardest for you to trust in God's plan for you, as Mary did? What can help you at such times?

Child When is it hardest for you to obey a parent or teacher? What can help you obey with more trust?

CHRISTMASTIME THEME: THE OBEDIENCE OF FAITH

The readings and questions for Christmas Day can be found in the Seasonal Feasts section at the end of this year.

Holy Family Respect for elders

Reading I Sirach 3:2–6, 12–14 (duties toward parents)

Reading II Colossians 3:12–21 (the practice of virtues)

Gospel Luke 2:41–52 (the finding in the temple)

Key Passage Jesus went down with them and came to Nazareth, and was obedient to them. (Luke 2:51a)

Adult What does your family do to honor and respect its older members?

Child Why did Jesus leave the temple? How can Jesus be an example for you?

Mary, Mother of God Living with uncertainty

Reading I Numbers 6:22–27 (the priestly blessing)

Reading II Galatians 4:4–7 (free sons of God in Christ)

Gospel Luke 2:16–21 (the shepherds' visit, the circumcision)

Key Passage Mary treasured all these words and pondered them in her heart. (Luke 2:19)

Adult When have you found it difficult to understand or accept a teaching of the church? What helps you be faithful?

Child Who teaches you to have faith in God?

Epiphany Overcoming jealousy

Reading I Isaiah 60:1–6 (glory of the new Zion)

Reading II Ephesians 3:2–3, 5–6 (commission to preach God's plan)

Gospel Matthew 2:1–12 (the visit of the magi)

Key Passage Then Herod sent the [magi] to Bethlehem, saying, "Go and search diligently for the child; and when you have found him bring me word so that I may also go and pay him homage." (Matthew 2:8)

Adult When have you been jealous or fearful of another person? When are such feelings harmful?

Child When have you been jealous because something good happened to another person instead of you? What is the problem with feeling that way?

Baptism of the Lord Pleasing to God

Reading I Isaiah 42:1–4, 6–7 (the servant of the Lord)

Reading II Acts 10:34–38 (Peter's discourse; the good news of peace)

Gospel Luke 3:15–16, 21–22 (baptism of Jesus)

Key Passage And a voice came from heaven, "You are my Son, the Beloved; with you I am well pleased." (Luke 3:2)

Adult Do you think that God was "well pleased" by your actions in recent weeks? Why?

Child What good thing could you do this week that would be pleasing to God?

LENTEN THEME: VIRTUOUS LIVING

Questions for Ash Wednesday can be found in the Seasonal Feasts section at the end of this year.

First Sunday of Lent Salvation through faith

Reading I Deuteronomy 26:4–10 (thanksgiving for the Lord's goodness)

Reading II Romans 10:8–13 (the faith of the Christian)

Gospel Luke 4:1–13 (temptation in the desert)

Key Passage For "everyone who calls on the name of the Lord shall be saved." (Romans 10:13)

Adult How willing are you to profess your faith in Jesus Christ openly to others?

Child Would you still be able to say that you believe in Jesus if others made fun of you for it?

Second Sunday of Lent Transformed by Christ

Reading I Genesis 15:5–12, 17–18 (the covenant with Abram)

Reading II Philippians 3:17—4:1 (Christ our goal)

Gospel Luke 9:28b–36 (Jesus transfigured)

Key Passage But our citizenship is in heaven, and it is from there that we are expecting a Savior, the Lord Jesus Christ. (Philippians 3:20)

Adult How are your priorities affected by your faith in Jesus Christ?

Child When you have important choices to make, do you and your family pray to make the right choice?

Third Sunday of Lent Tempered with humility

Reading I Exodus 3:1–8b, 13–15 (the call of Moses)

Reading II 1 Corinthians 10:1–6, 10–12 (against overconfidence)

Gospel Luke 13:1–19 (calls to penance; parables of the reign of God)

Key Passage The reign of God is like a mustard seed that someone took and sowed in the garden; it grew and became a tree, and the birds of the air made nests in its branches. (Luke 13:19b)

Adult What important work could bear fruit in your life right now if you have more confidence in God's loving care?

Child What great work would you like to do as you grow older? What can you do to begin now?

Fourth Sunday of Lent A generous spirit

Reading I Joshua 5:9a, 10–12 (rites at Gilgal)

Reading II 2 Corinthians 5:17–21 (a new creation)

Gospel Luke 15:1–3, 11b–32 (the prodigal son)

Key Passage Then the father said to him, "Son, you are always with me, and all that is mine is yours. But we had to celebrate and rejoice, because this brother of yours was dead and has come to life; he was lost and has been found." (Luke 15:31–32)

Adult When have you been generous enough to forgive someone who hurt you deeply?

Child Is there someone you need to forgive or ask forgiveness of?

Fifth Sunday of Lent False pride

Reading I Isaiah 43:16–21 (promise of restoration)

Reading II Philippians 3:8–14 (breaking with the past)

Gospel John 8:1–11 (the adulteress)

Key Passage Jesus straightened up and said, "Let anyone among you who is without sin be the first to throw a stone at her." (John 8:7)

Adult Have you ever been too willing to "cast the first stone" when you disapproved of someone's behavior? How can you resist these feelings?

Child When have you criticized or made fun of someone? What could help you act differently?

Passion (Palm) Sunday Love and betrayal

Reading I Isaiah 50:4–7 (salvation only through the Lord's servant)

Reading II Philippians 2:6–11 (imitating Christ's humility)

Gospel Luke 22:14—23:56 (the passion of Jesus)

Key Passage The Lord turned and looked at Peter. Then Peter remembered the word of the Lord, how he had said to him, "Before the cock crows today, you will deny me three times." (Luke 22:61)

Adult When have you felt that you betrayed the confidence of another, as Peter did when he denied Jesus?

Child When have you let someone down who trusted you? How did you feel?

TRIDUUM THEME: LIFE POURED OUT FOR OTHERS

Holy Thursday Called to serve

Reading I Exodus 12:1–8, 11–14 (the Passover ritual prescribed)

Reading II 1 Corinthians 11:23–26 (the Lord's Supper)

Gospel John 13:1–15 (the washing of the feet)

Key Passage Jesus said, "If I, your Lord and Teacher, have washed your feet, you also ought to wash one another's feet. For I have set you an example, that you also should do as I have done to you." (John 13:14–15)

Adult What is the most difficult thing you have done as a service to another person?

Child What is the hardest thing you have ever done for another person who needed your help?

Good Friday Perfection through suffering

Reading I Isaiah 52:13—53:12 (suffering and triumph of the servant of the Lord)

Reading II Hebrews 4:14–16; 5:7–9 (Jesus, compassionate high priest)

Gospel John 18:1—19:42 (the passion of our Lord Jesus Christ)

Key Passage When you make his life an offering for sin, he shall see his offspring, and shall prolong his days; through him the will of the Lord shall prosper. (Isaiah 53:10)

Adult Can you say that you have grown through your experiences of physical or emotional suffering? Why or why not?

Child How can the story of Jesus' suffering make it easier for you to face something painful or uncomfortable?

Holy Saturday (Vigil) New life in Christ

Reading I Genesis 1:1—2:2 (first story of creation)

Reading II Genesis 22:1–18 (the testing of Abraham)

Reading III Exodus 14:15—15:1 (crossing of the Red Sea and destruction of the Egyptians)

Reading IV Isaiah 54:5–14 (the new Zion)

Reading V Isaiah 55:1–11 (an invitation to grace)

Reading VI Baruch 3:9–15, 32—4:4 (wisdom prayer in the Law of Moses)

Reading VII Ezekiel 36:16–17a, 18–28 (regeneration of the people)

Epistle Romans 6:3–11 (death to sin, life in God)

Gospel Luke 24:1–12 (the women at the tomb)

Key Passage Therefore we have been buried with him by baptism into death, so that, just as Christ was raised from the dead by the glory of the Father, so we too might walk in newness of life. (Romans 6:4)

Adult What benefits has the new life of baptism brought to your life?

Child If someone who was not a Christian asked you what difference it makes to be baptized, what would you say?

EASTERTIME THEME: NEW LIFE IN CHRIST

Easter Sunday Made new by Christ

Reading I Acts 10:34, 37–43 (Peter's discourse)

Reading II Colossians 3:1–4 (mystical death and resurrection). Or 1 Corinthians 5:6–8 (the yeast of sincerity and truth)

Gospel John 20:1–9 (Peter and the disciple at the tomb)

Key Passage Clean out the old yeast so that you may be a new batch, as you really are unleavened. For our paschal lamb, Christ, has been sacrificed. (1 Corinthians 5:7)

Adult What change could the hope of the resurrection of Christ inspire you to make?

Child What bad habit would you like to "clear out" during the hopeful time of this Easter season?

Second Sunday of Easter Living without fear

Reading I Acts 5:12–16 (signs and wonders)

Reading II Revelation 1:9–11a, 12–13, 17–19 (first vision)

Gospel John 20:19–31 (appearance to the disciples; Thomas)

Key Passage He placed his right hand on me, saying, "Do not be afraid; I am the first and the last, and the living one. I was dead, and see, I am alive forever and ever." (Revelation 1:17b–18a)

Adult When has your faith in the living Christ helped you overcome fear?

Child What could you do this Easter season to help someone feel less afraid?

Third Sunday of Easter Feed my sheep

Reading I Acts 5:27b–32, 40b–41 (disciples' second trial before the Sanhedrin)

Reading II Revelation 5:11–14 (praise to the Lamb)

Gospel John 21:1–19 (appearance at the Sea of Tiberias)

Key Passage When they had finished breakfast, Jesus said to Simon Peter, "Simon son of John, do you love me more than these?" He said to him, "Yes, Lord; you know that I love you." Jesus said to him, "Feed my lambs." (John 21:15)

Adult In what ways are you answering Jesus' command to Peter to "feed my sheep"?

Child What do you do to take care of others as Jesus asked Peter to do?

Fourth Sunday of Easter Protected by Christ

Reading I Acts 13:14, 43–52 (Paul's and Barnabas' address to the Gentiles)

Reading II Revelation 7:9, 14–17 (rejoicing of the elect of every nation)

Gospel John 10:27–30 (words at the feast of the dedication of the temple)

Key Passage Jesus said, "My sheep hear my voice. I know them, and they follow me. I give them eternal life, and they will never perish. No one will snatch them out of my hand." (John 10:27–28)

Adult Whom do you try to protect as Christ protects you?

Child Who helps you feel safe and protected? Whom can you take care of and help feel safe?

Fifth Sunday of Easter Love one another

Reading I Acts 14:21–27 (end of the first mission)

Reading II Revelation 21:1–5a (new heavens and new earth)

Gospel John 13:31–33a, 34–35 (a new commandment)

Key Passage Jesus said, "I give you a new commandment, that you love one another. Just as I have loved you, you also should love one another." (John 13:34)

Adult When have you seen the power of love overcome a bad situation?

Child Do you believe love is stronger than hate? Why?

Sixth Sunday of Easter Keeping Jesus' word

Reading I Acts 15:1–2, 22–29 (letter of the Apostles to the Gentiles)

Reading II Revelation 21:10–14, 22–23 (the new Jerusalem)

Gospel John 14:23–29 (last discourse; faithfulness to God's word)

Key Passage Jesus answered him, "Those who love me will keep my word, and my Father will love them, and we will come to them and make our home with them." (John 14:23)

Adult What difference has it made in your life when you made a decision in accord with Jesus' teachings?

Child When will you have to make a decision this week? What will help you make a good decision?

Seventh Sunday of Easter Prayer for others

Reading I Acts 7:55–60 (Stephen's martyrdom)

Reading II Revelation 22:12–14, 16–17, 20 (blessed are those who follow the Lamb)

Gospel John 17:20–26 (prayer for all believers)

Key Passage Jesus prayed, "I pray not only for them, but also for those who will believe in me through their word, so that they may all be one, as you, Father, are in me and I in you, that they also may be in us, that the world may believe that you sent me." (John 18:20–21)

Adult What are some of the most important things to ask of God?

Child What are some of the most important things to ask of God?

Pentecost Gifts for service

Reading I Acts 2:1–11 (descent of the Holy Spirit)

Reading II 1 Corinthians 12:3–7, 12–13 (many gifts, one Spirit, and the analogy of the body)

Gospel John 20:19–23 (appearance to the disciples)

Key Passage Now there are varieties of gifts, but the same Spirit; and there are varieties of services, but the same Lord. (1 Corinthians 12:4–5)

Adult What gift of service have you received from the Holy Spirit and how well are you using it right now?

Child What gift do you hope to receive from the Holy Spirit? How could you use it to serve others?

ORDINARY TIME THEME 1: A SPIRIT OF RESPONSIBILITY

Trinity Sunday The Spirit of truth

Reading I Proverbs 8:22–31 (the discourse of wisdom)

Reading II Romans 5:1–5 (faith, hope, and love)

Gospel John 16:12–15 (coming of the Paraclete)

Key Passage Jesus said, "I still have many things to say to you, but you cannot bear them now. When the Spirit of truth comes, he will guide you into all the truth; for he will not speak on his own, but will speak whatever he hears, and he will declare to you the things that are to come." (John 16:12–13a)

Adult In what difficult situation has the Holy Spirit helped you see more clearly?

Child What kind of decision can the Holy Spirit help you with?

Body and Blood of Christ Service to others

Reading I Genesis 14:18–20 (Melchizedek's blessing of Abram)

Reading II 1 Corinthians 11:23–26 (the Lord's Supper)

Gospel Luke 9:11b–17 (multiplication of the loaves)

Key Passage For I received from the Lord what I also handed on to you, that the Lord Jesus on the night when he was betrayed took a loaf of bread, and when he had given thanks, he broke it and said, "This is my body that is for you. Do this in remembrance of me." (1 Corinthians 11:23–24)

Adult When have you been most blessed and when have you felt a little "broken" in your service to others?

Child Why is it important to keep on giving, even when you are tired?

Second Sunday in Ordinary Time Thinking of others

Reading I Isaiah 62:1–5 (Jerusalem the Lord's bride)

Reading II 1 Corinthians 12:4–11 (variety and unity)

Gospel John 2:1–12 (the wedding at Cana)

Key Passage When the wine gave out, the mother of Jesus said to him, "They have no wine." (John 2:3)

Adult When have you stepped in, as Mary did at Cana, to try and make a difficult situation easier for someone?

Child What can you do this week to help make someone's job a little easier?

Third Sunday in Ordinary Time Accepting responsibility

Reading I Nehemiah 8:2b–4a, 5–6, 8–10 (Ezra reads the Law)

Reading II 1 Corinthians 12:12–30 (analogy of the body)

Gospel Luke 1:1–4; 4:14–21 (beginning of Jesus' preaching)

Key Passage Jesus unrolled the scroll and found the place where it was written: "The Spirit of the Lord is upon me, because he has anointed me to bring good news to the poor." (Luke 4:17b–18a)

Adult What do you believe that the anointing you received at baptism requires you to do?

Child What could you do this week for someone who has less than you?

Fourth Sunday in Ordinary Time Facing rejection

Reading I Jeremiah 1:4–5, 17–19 (prophet consecrated to God)

Reading II 1 Corinthians 12:31—13:13 (love never fails)

Gospel Luke 4:21–30 (beginning of preaching; rejection by the townspeople)

Key Passage They got up, drove him out of the town, and led him to the brow of the hill on which their town was built, so that they might hurl him off the cliff. But he passed through the midst of them and went on his way. (Luke 4:29–30)

Adult What do you do when a message you are trying to deliver "falls on deaf ears"?

Child Are there times when you have not listened as well as you could to what someone was telling you? Why didn't you?

Fifth Sunday in Ordinary Time Stretching our limits

Reading I Isaiah 6:1–2a, 3–8 (call of Isaiah)

Reading II 1 Corinthians 15:1–11 (Christ's resurrection)

Gospel Luke 5:1b–11 (call of the first disciples)

Key Passage Simon Peter fell down at Jesus' knees, saying, "Go away from me, Lord, for I am a sinful man." Then Jesus said to Simon, "Do not be afraid; from now on you will be catching people." (Luke 5:8,10b)

Adult When have you felt inadequate to a task or role you were given? How did you respond?

Child When have you been asked to do something you felt might be too hard for you? What did you do?

ORDINARY TIME THEME 2: LOVE OF NEIGHBOR

Sixth Sunday in Ordinary Time Reaching out to others

Reading I 1 Jeremiah 17:5–8 (true wisdom)

Reading II 1 Corinthians 15:12, 16–20 (the resurrection and faith)

Gospel Luke 6:17, 20–26 (the great discourse)

Key Passage Then he looked up at his disciples and said: "Blessed are you who are poor, for yours is the kingdom of God." (Luke 6:20)

Adult In what way are you serving the poor, as Jesus did?

Child When have you helped bring God's love to someone who was sad, or hungry, or whom others made fun of?

Seventh Sunday in Ordinary Time In another's shoes

Reading I 1 Samuel 26:2, 7–9, 12–13, 22–23 (Saul's life spared; Saul admits his guilt)

Reading II 1 Corinthians 15:45–49 (the natural and the spiritual body)

Gospel Luke 6:27–38 (love of one's enemy)

Key Passage Jesus said, "But I say to you that listen, Love your enemies, do good to those who hate you, bless those who curse you, pray for those who abuse you." (Luke 6:27–28)

Adult What has allowed you to overcome obstacles and forgive someone who has hurt you?

Child When has it been hard to forgive someone who hurt you? What did you do?

Eighth Sunday in Ordinary Time Authentic living

Reading I Sirach 27:4–7 (all tested by their speech)

Reading II 1 Corinthians 15:54–58 (glorification of the body)

Gospel Luke 6:39–45 (all known by their works)

Key Passage Jesus said, "How can you say to your neighbor, 'Friend, let me take out the speck in your eye,' when you yourself do not see the log in your own eye?" (Luke 6:42a)

Adult When have you most felt like a hypocrite? How did you overcome this feeling?

Child Is it a good thing or a bad thing to act differently from what you are really feeling? Explain.

Ninth Sunday in Ordinary Time The strength of God's love

Reading I 1 Kings 8:41–43 (dedication of the temple; welcome of the foreigner)

Reading II Galatians 1:1–2, 6–10 (reproof for disloyalty)

Gospel Luke 7:1–10 (cure of the centurion's servant)

Key Passage The centurion sent friends to say to him, "Lord, do not trouble yourself, for I am not worthy to have you come under my roof; therefore I did not presume to come to you. But only speak the word, and let my servant be healed." (Luke 7:6b–7)

Adult When have you experienced most powerfully that the Lord was helping you in a time of need?

Child What good things has God done for you?

ORDINARY TIME THEME 3: SOURCE OF CONSOLATION

Tenth Sunday in Ordinary Time Moved with pity

Reading I 1 Kings 17:17–24 (Elijah and the widow)

Reading II Galatians 1:11–19 (Paul called by Christ)

Gospel Luke 7:11–17 (the widow's son)

Key Passage As Jesus approached the gate of the town, a man who had died was being carried out. He was his mother's only son, and she was a widow; and with her was a large crowd from the town. When the Lord saw her, he had compassion for her and said to her, "Do not weep." (Luke 7:12–13)

Adult What might a greater sense of compassion allow you to do for someone this week?

Child When did you try to understand what another person was feeling?

Eleventh Sunday in Ordinary Time The courage to forgive

Reading I 2 Samuel 12:7–10, 13 (David's punishment and repentance)

Reading II Galatians 2:16, 19–21 (Paul's basic teaching)

Gospel Luke 7:36—8:3 (the penitent woman)

Key Passage Then Jesus said to her, "Your sins are forgiven." But those who were at the table with him began to say among themselves, "Who is this who even forgives sins?" (Luke 7:48–49)

Adult Whom does your Christian faith call you to forgive right now? How hard will this be for you?

Child When is it hard for you to forgive someone who has hurt you? What can help you forgive?

Twelfth Sunday in Ordinary Time Calming life's storms

Reading I Zechariah 12:10–11 (messianic Jerusalem)

Reading II Galatians 3:26–29 (one in Christ Jesus)

Gospel Luke 9:18–24 (followers of Jesus)

Key Passage Then Jesus said to them all, "If any want to become my followers, let them deny themselves and take up their cross daily and follow me." (Luke 9:23)

Adult Which crosses in your life do you find especially heavy? What or who helps you bear them?

Child When you have something hard to do, what or who helps you get through it?

Thirteenth Sunday in Ordinary Time Don't look back

Reading I 1 Kings 19:16b, 19–21 (call of Elisha)

Reading II Galatians 5:1, 13–18 (proper use of freedom)

Gospel Luke 9:51–62 (the apostles' requirements)

Key Passage Another said, "I will follow you, Lord; but let me first say farewell to those at my home." Jesus said to him, "No one who puts a hand to the plow and looks back is fit for the kingdom of God." (Luke 9:61–62)

Adult When have you faltered or looked back during your journey of faith?

Child What can you do to be a stronger follower of Jesus this week?

Fourteenth Sunday in Ordinary Time Accepting the Christian message

Reading I Isaiah 66:10–14 (mother Zion)

Reading II Galatians 6:14–18 (the cross, our true boast)

Gospel Luke 10:1–12, 17–20 (mission of the seventy–two)

Key Passage Jesus said to the disciples, "Whenever you enter a town and they do not welcome you, go out into its streets and say, 'Even the dust of your town that clings to our feet, we wipe off in protest against you. Yet know this: the kingdom of God has come near.'" (Luke 10:10–11)

Adult Where do you see the message of Christian faith being rejected in the world today? What is your response to that?

Child What can you do when you are generous with others, and they do not want what you give them?

Fifteenth Sunday in Ordinary Time Acting with mercy

Reading I Deuteronomy 30:10–14 (God's command clear)

Reading II Colossians 1:15–20 (Christ's fullness and reconciliation)

Gospel Luke 10:25–37 (the good Samaritan)

Key Passage But a Samaritan while traveling came near him; and when he saw him, he was moved with pity. He went to him and bandaged his wounds, having poured oil and wine on them. Then he put him on his own animal, brought him to an inn, and took care of him. (Luke 10:33–34)

Adult When have you gone out of your way to help a stranger in need?

Child Would you help a new student who needed help? Why or why not?

ORDINARY TIME THEME 4: BALANCING PRAYER AND ACTION

Sixteenth Sunday in Ordinary Time

Reading I Genesis 18:1–10a (Abraham's visitors)

Reading II Colossians 1:24–28 (the mystery: Christ in us)

Gospel Luke 10:38–42 (Martha and Mary)

Key Passage Jesus said to Martha, "There is need of only one thing. Mary has chosen the better part, which will not be taken away from her." (Luke 10:42)

Adult Which response to God's call is more natural to you—prayer or action? Why?

Child In the past week, when have you prayed and when have you done good things for others? Which could you do better?

Seventeenth Sunday in Ordinary Time Daily prayer

Reading I Genesis 18:20–32 (Abraham intercedes for Sodom)

Reading II Colossians 2:12–14 (sovereign role of Christ)

Gospel Luke 11:1–13 (the Our Father)

Key Passage Jesus said, "So I say to you, Ask, and it will be given you; search, and you will find; knock, and the door will be opened for you." (Luke 11:9)

Adult Have your most recent prayers been prayers of praise, petition, or sorrow? Which kind of prayer do you need to practice more often?

Child What are you most thankful for right now?

Eighteenth Sunday in Ordinary Time Seeking balance

Reading I Ecclesiastes 1:2; 2:21–23 (on vanity)

Reading II Colossians 3:1–5, 9–11 (mystical death and resurrection)

Gospel Luke 12:13–21 (trust in God, not in possessions)

Key Passage And Jesus said to them, "Take care! Be on your guard against all kinds of greed; for one's life does not consist in the abundance of possessions." (Luke 12:15)

Adult When have you felt that possessions were becoming too important in your life?

Child Have you ever received a gift you wanted a lot and then found it didn't make you as happy as you thought it would?

Nineteenth Sunday in Ordinary Time Running the race of faith

Reading I Wisdom 18:6–9a (on the death of the Egyptian first-born)

Reading II Hebrews 11:1–2, 8–19 (faith of the ancients)

Gospel Luke 12:32–48 (dependence on Providence; preparedness for the master's return)

Key Passage Therefore, since we are surrounded by so great a cloud of witnesses, let us also lay aside every weight and the sin that clings so closely, and let us run with perseverance the race that is set before us, looking to Jesus the pioneer and perfecter of our faith. (Hebrews 12:1–2a)

Adult Other than Jesus, which of the ancestors of Christian faith has served as the greatest example to you? Why?

Child Which person of the Bible has been a good example to you of how to live?

ORDINARY TIME THEME 5: THE CHALLENGES OF CHRISTIANITY

Twentieth Sunday in Ordinary Time An unsettling truth

Reading I Jeremiah 38:4–6, 8–10 (Jeremiah in the miry cistern)

Reading II Hebrews 12:1–4 (God's treatment of his sons and daughters)

Gospel Luke 12:49–53 (Jesus' mission of division)

Key Passage Jesus said, "Do you think that I have come to bring peace to the earth? No, I tell you, but rather division!" (Luke 12:51)

Adult When has your taking a strong stand on a moral issue created division rather than healing in the short term?

Child Is it important to do the right thing even if others are angry as a result? Why or why not?

Twenty-first Sunday in Ordinary Time The narrow door

Reading I Isaiah 66:18–21 (gathering of the nations)

Reading II Hebrews 12:5–7, 11–13 (the discipline of God)

Gospel Luke 13:22–30 (the narrow door)

Key Passage Jesus answered them, "Strive to enter through the narrow door; for many, I tell you, will try to enter and will not be able." (Luke 13:24)

Adult What daily choices are you making that will allow you to be recognized at the doorway of the reign of God?

Child What good habits are you practicing in order to be a good Christian?

Twenty-second Sunday in Ordinary Time Seeking humility

Reading I Sirach 3:17–18, 20, 28–29 (humility)

Reading II Hebrews 12:18–19, 22–24a (God the judge; Jesus the mediator)

Gospel Luke 14:1, 7–14 (a lesson in humility)

Key Passage Jesus said, "But when you give a banquet, invite the poor, the crippled, the lame, and the blind. And you will be blessed, because they cannot repay you, for you will be repaid at the resurrection of the righteous." (Luke 14:13–14)

Adult Has the hunger for status and influence in the world around you endangered your life as a Christian?

Child Does it make you a better person to be chosen first for a team or some other honor? Why or why not?

Twenty-third Sunday in Ordinary Time Discerning God's will

Reading I Wisdom 9:13–18a (Solomon's prayer)

Reading II Philemon 9b–10, 12–17 (plea for Onesimus)

Gospel Luke 14:25–33 (sayings on discipleship)

Key Passage For who can learn the counsel of God? Or who can discern what the Lord wills? For the reasoning of mortals is worthless, and our designs are likely to fail. (Wisdom 9:13–14)

Adult How do you try to discover what God is asking of you?

Child When is it hard for you to know the right thing to do? Who helps you know?

Twenty-fourth Sunday in Ordinary Time The courage to forgive

Reading I Exodus 32:7–11, 13–14 (the golden calf)

Reading II 1 Timothy 1:12–17 (Paul's gratitude)

Gospel Luke 15:1–32 (the prodigal son)

Key Passage The servant replied, "Your brother has come, and your father has killed the fatted calf, because he has got him back safe and sound." Then he became angry and refused to go in. His father came out and began to plead with him. (Luke 15:27–28)

Adult When have you persistently sought after a member of your family who has lost his or her way?

Child Have you ever felt you were not getting credit for your good works? What did you do?

ORDINARY TIME THEME 6: THE FAITHFUL CHRISTIAN

Twenty-fifth Sunday in Ordinary Time The value of honesty

Reading I Amos 8:4–7 (against greed)

Reading II 1 Timothy 2:1–8 (conduct of men and women)

Gospel Luke 16:1–13 (the dishonest steward)

Key Passage Whoever is faithful in a very little is faithful also in much; and whoever is dishonest in a very little is dishonest also in much. (Luke 16:10)

Adult Can cheating and deception ever be justified?

Child If someone treats you unfairly, do you have the right to do the same to them?

Twenty-sixth Sunday in Ordinary Time The rich and the poor

Reading I Amos 6:1a, 4–7 (third woe)

Reading II 1 Timothy 6:11–16 (the good fight of faith)

Gospel Luke 16:19–31 (the rich man and Lazarus)

Key Passage There was a rich man who was dressed in purple and fine linen and who feasted sumptuously every day. And at his gate lay a poor man named Lazarus, covered with sores, who longed to satisfy his hunger with what fell from the rich man's table. (Luke 16:19–21)

Adult What are the "rewards" of caring for the needs of the poor?

Child What is one thing you and your family could do this week to help those who are poor or sick?

Twenty-seventh Sunday in Ordinary Time Faithful Christians

Reading I Habakkuk 1:2–3; 2:2–4a (Habakkuk's complaint)

Reading II 2 Timothy 1:6–8, 13–14 (exhortation to faithfulness)

Gospel Luke 17:5–10 (sayings on the requirements of faith)

Key Passage Jesus said, "So you also, when you have done all that you were ordered to do, say, 'We are worthless slaves; we have done only what we ought to have done!'" (Luke 17:10)

Adult When have you done more than was required of you in the service of others?

Child When have you done something extra for someone in your family without being asked? What did you learn from this?

Twenty-eighth Sunday in Ordinary Time Saying thank you

Reading I 2 Kings 5:14–17 (Elisha's cure of Naaman)

Reading II 2 Timothy 2:8–13 (Paul's faithfulness to the gospel)

Gospel Luke 17:11–19 (ten lepers)

Key Passage Then one of the lepers, when he saw that he was healed, turned back, praising God with a loud voice. He prostrated himself at Jesus' feet and thanked him. And he was a Samaritan. (Luke 17:15–16)

Adult Whose generosity do you tend to take for granted? How will you change this?

Child When have you failed to say thank you? Why does this matter?

Twenty-ninth Sunday in Ordinary Time Taking responsibility

Reading I Exodus 17:8–13 (battle with Amalek)

Reading II 2 Timothy 3:14—4:2 (apostolic charge)

Gospel Luke 18:1–8 (the corrupt judge)

Key Passage For a while the judge refused; but later he said to himself, "Though I have no fear of God and no respect for anyone, yet because this widow keeps bothering me, I will grant her justice, so that she may not wear me out by continually coming." (Luke 18:4–5)

Adult Whose needs might you be failing to listen to right now?

Child How often do you put off chores until you are forced to do them? Who is hurt by such a decision?

Thirtieth Sunday in Ordinary Time The reward of humility

Reading I Sirach 35:12–14, 16–18 (the God of justice)

Reading II 2 Timothy 4:6–8, 16–18 (reward for fidelity)

Gospel Luke 18:9–14 (the Pharisee and the tax collector)

Key Passage Jesus said, "I tell you, this man went down to his home justified rather than the other; for all who exalt themselves will be humbled, but all who humble themselves will be exalted." (Luke 18:14)

Adult When have you felt self-satisfied in observing the mistakes of others? What should we remember at such times?

Child Have you ever thought you were better than someone else? What is the problem with such thoughts?

ORDINARY TIME THEME 7: BRINGING PEACE

Thirty-first Sunday in Ordinary Time Welcoming the sinner

Reading I Wisdom 11:22—12:1 (digression on God's mercy)

Reading II 2 Thessalonians 1:11—2:2 (exhortation to faithfulness)

Gospel Luke 19:1–10 (Zacchaeus the tax collector)

Key Passage And Jesus said to Zacchaeus, "Today salvation has come to this house, because he too is a son of Abraham. For the Son of Man came to seek out and to save the lost." (Luke 19:9–10)

Adult During the next week, what could you do to welcome someone who usually feels excluded?

Child Is there a child in your class or neighborhood who is left out of games and activities? What can you do?

Thirty-second Sunday in Ordinary Time The dead will rise

Reading I 2 Maccabees 7:1–2, 9–14 (martyrdom of a mother and her sons)

Reading II 2 Thessalonians 2:16—3:5 (the gospel versus empty fables)

Gospel Luke 20:27–38 (the resurrection of the dead)

Key Passage Jesus said, "And the fact that the dead are raised Moses himself showed, in the story about the bush, where he speaks of the Lord as the God of Abraham, the God of Isaac, and the God of Jacob. Now he is God not of the dead, but of the living; for to him all of them are alive." (Luke 20:37–38)

Adult How does your belief in the resurrection of the dead affect the way you live?

Child Has someone in your family or among your friends died? Do you think about that person in heaven? What do you hope to talk about with this person?

Thirty-third Sunday in Ordinary Time Overcoming difficulties

Reading I Malachi 3:19–20a (messenger of the covenant)

Reading II 2 Thessalonians 3:7–12 (qualifications of various ministers)

Gospel Luke 21:5–19 (the cataclysm to come)

Key Passage Jesus said, "You will be hated by all because of my name. But not a hair of your head will perish. By your endurance you will gain your souls." (Luke 21:17–19)

Adult When bad things happen, how do you deal with them?

Child Have you ever worried about something that might happen? What can help you worry less?

Christ the King True authority

Reading I 2 Samuel 5:1–3 (David king of Israel)

Reading II Colossians 1:12–20 (Christ's fullness and reconciliation)

Gospel Luke 23:35–43 (the crucifixion; the king of the Jews)

Key Passage For in him all the fullness of God was pleased to dwell, and through him God was pleased to reconcile to himself all things, whether on earth or in heaven, by making peace through the blood of his cross. (Colossians 1:19–20)

Adult Following the example of Jesus, what is the best way to exercise your authority over others?

Child What qualities would a good leader have? Which of these are you trying to develop?

SEASONAL FEASTS

Immaculate Conception

Reading I Genesis 3:9–15, 20 (the fall)

Reading II Ephesians 1:3–6, 11–12 (the Father's plan for salvation)

Gospel Luke 1:26–38 (announcement of the birth of Jesus)

Key Passage Ephesians 1:4 (chosen by God)

Adult How has faith in Jesus transformed your life?

Child Who in your family has helped you have faith in Jesus?

Christmas Day

Reading I Isaiah 52:7–10 (the one who brings glad tidings)

Reading II Hebrews 1:1–6 (God speaks through his Son)

Gospel John 1:1–18 (in the beginning was the Word)

Key Passage John 1:10–11 ("His own did not accept him")

Adult If Jesus were to be born today, do you think you would accept him and follow him? Why or why not?

Child What could you and your family do for others during the next week to celebrate the birth of Jesus?

Ash Wednesday

Reading I Joel 2:12–18 (the merciful God)

Reading II 2 Corinthians 5:20—6:2 (the day of salvation)

Gospel Matthew 6:1–6, 16–18 (purity of intention)

Key Passage 2 Corinthians 6:2 (the day of salvation)

Adult What good work can you do during this Lent that you have not taken time to do before?

Child What could you and your family do during Lent to help bring the good news to someone else?

Ascension

Reading I Acts 1:1–11 (Jesus' final instructions and ascension)

Reading II Ephesians 1:17–23 (a Spirit of wisdom)

Gospel Luke 24:46–53 (the ascension)

Key Passage Ephesians 1:17 (a Spirit of wisdom)

Adult Who in your family has the gift of wisdom? How does he or she use this gift?

Child Who is the wisest person you know? What has he or she taught you?

Assumption: Vigil

Reading I 1 Chronicles 15:3–4, 15; 16:1–2 (the ark brought to Jerusalem)

Reading II 1 Corinthians 15:54–57 (glorification of the body)

Gospel Luke 11:27–28 (true happiness by keeping the word of God)

Key Passage 1 Corinthians 15:54 ("Death has been swallowed up in victory")

Adult How does your belief in external life affect your daily life?

Child What does it mean to have hope?

All Saints

Reading I Revelation 7:2–4, 9–14 (rejoicing of the elect)

Reading II 1 John 3:1–3 (children of God)

Gospel Matthew 5:1–12 (the beatitudes)

Key Passage 1 John 3:1 (children of God)

Adult What qualities do you see in yourself that mark you as a child of God?

Child What is good about being a child of God?

Session Theme Outlines for Year A

YEAR C, INTRODUCTORY THEME: THE JOURNEY OF FAITH

Once your parish community has become comfortable with reflections on the Questions of the Week, they will begin to ask you for a next step. This chapter suggests a model you could use. Except for this introductory theme, it is based on Year A of the lectionary, using the double-spiral approach suggested in Chapter 3. You can use these outlines to develop a simple one- or two-hour session plan. You might invite parishioners to attend these sessions after one of the Sunday liturgies for four weeks during each liturgical season.

If your parish is just beginning adult faith formation, or whole community catechesis, you may decide to begin by offering the sessions only during Advent and Lent. If the program is successful, add several more sessions each year, until your parish is meeting during each of the seasons of the church year.

Life Connections

Each participant in this series will experience the readings, presentations, and questions according to his or her own age and life situation. Here are some predictable attitudes and feelings that might arise for some, especially adults, during group conversations:

- Disappointing or conflicted home situations
- Reticence to share personal family stories
- Negative or limiting images of God
- Anger with God over certain life events

- Lack of understanding of the Bible
- Misunderstanding of church teaching
- Discomfort with or excessive docility to church authority

Introduction

This series is a good starting point for parish members entering a process of adult faith formation for the first time. It gives family members of all ages the opportunity to reflect together on their faith journey. Offer this series each fall, preceding Advent, to first-time participants. You could offer the four topics in this series either in separate sessions, or as part of a half day or full day. Participants will examine the family context in which they live their faith and reflect on their current relationship with God. They'll uncover the ways that God speaks to them in time and space. They'll learn more about the ways in which God's revelation to others has been passed on through Scripture and tradition and is still speaking to them today.

SESSION TOPICS

1. Households of Faith

Seasonal Lectionary Connection: Year C

Twenty-seventh Sunday in Ordinary Time

Luke 17:5–10 (the requirements of faith)

Presentation Overview

Some of us experienced the beginnings of faith within loving, supportive Christian families. Others first learned of God's love from relatives outside their homes. For others, living faith was missing at home, and they first came to faith in school or religious education settings. Some were much older before they felt the first stirrings of faith. However, probably all who choose to attend this series dream of living in vibrant, faith-filled households that either reflect or improve upon the experience of their childhood. This first topic allows individuals to name and reflect upon their unique experiences as family and to strengthen the bonds that connect them to one another and to God.

References: *Catechism of the Catholic Church* or CCC, 1655–1657.

Sample Dialogue Questions

- Who lives in your household of faith?
- Are all the members of your household of the same faith tradition? What difference does this make?
- What are your family's favorite religious practices and traditions?

Psalm Prayer

Psalm 90 (God's eternity and our frailty)

2. Yearning for God

Seasonal Lectionary Connection: Year C

Sixteenth Sunday in Ordinary Time

Luke 10:38–42 (Martha and Mary)

Presentation Overview

This second topic will help participants reflect on their past and present faith. Many of us experienced our first glimmerings of the transcendent God as young children through the wonder and awe we felt observing the beauty and complexity of creation. We first came to know the intimacy of God's love through the unconditional love we received from parents or other caregivers. The gift of God's grace is that, even if we were deprived of such early experiences, we are never too old to begin to encounter the creative power of God's love in our lives. For, in fact, God's yearning for us is active, constant, and overflowing.

We seek God because God has first sought us. The ways that we imagine and experience God's call to us varies from one age to another. Many in beginning groups may not name it as a call, but they have some sense of when they came to believe. For each of us, our first expression of gratitude and assent to God's invitation to love was the beginning of faith. Learning to notice and name these experiences as they deepen is important to growth in faith throughout our lives. References: CCC, 27–38.

Dialogue Questions

- What was your earliest image of God? How has your idea of God changed since then?
- Where and when do you feel closest to God?

- Who first helped you believe in God?
- What most challenges your faith in God?

Psalm Prayer

Psalm 40 (gratitude and prayer for help)

3. God Comes to Meet Us

Seasonal Lectionary Connection: Year C

Eighteenth Sunday in Ordinary Time

Isaiah 55:1–3 (an invitation to grace)

Presentation Overview

God the Creator is both completely transcendent and deeply intimate with us, speaking to us in time—in the context of our historical settings and cultures. All peoples experience God in the context of their own traditions and world-views. It is this rich diversity of perception that allows the mystery of God to be revealed more fully in every age.

The Hebrew people were the first to experience the immediacy of God's presence. When God spoke to Moses through the burning bush, Moses asked God, "What is your name?" When God replied, "I am who am," Yahweh, the Being from whom all being flows, was revealed. God's act at this historical moment revealed the constancy of God's saving presence.

But God's presence is also a challenge, and Moses at that moment was called to lead the people on a difficult journey into the promise of freedom. God's encounter with each of us today is, in fact, always a call to freedom. This third session invites participants to begin to identify this call for themselves.

References: CCC, 51–54, 205–209.

Dialogue Questions

- What in God's creation most fills you with wonder and awe?
- Who has shown God's love to you, either recently or in the past?
- When do you feel the closest to God?

Psalm Prayer

Psalm 145 (the greatness and goodness of God)

4. Handing on the Faith

Seasonal Lectionary Connection: Year C

Nineteenth Sunday in Ordinary Time

Hebrews 11: 1–2, 8–12 (faith of the ancients)

Presentation Overview

The ancient Israelites gradually came to understand that Yahweh had been with them in their history from the beginning. After telling the stories of God's mighty deeds orally for generations, the people began to record these stories. These Hebrew Scriptures, written under God's inspiration, formed the context for the full revelation of God that would come through Jesus Christ.

All Christians must come to know the Bible, both the Hebrew and Christian Scriptures, in order to fully encounter the mystery of God's loving plan. The Scriptures are complex, yet reveal with great clarity the story of salvation and the path God has provided for us to participate in its blessings. Learning the stories of our tradition, reading them prayerfully, and interpreting the Scriptures correctly are necessary tasks in faith formation.

The tradition of the church, rooted in God's revelation through Jesus Christ, is the guide to a correct understanding and interpretation of the Scriptures. The church takes the profound mysteries of faith and makes them accessible to each generation, reading the "signs of the times," and helping believers to connect them with the great story of faith.

This fourth topic should give participants some practical tools for understanding God's gradual revelation of the divine plan. They'll learn ways to use the Scriptures and tradition more effectively to guide their faith journeys, always taking the gospel of Jesus Christ as their source and goal.

References: CCC, 31–38.

Dialogue Questions

- To what extent is the Bible used in your family as a source of life and faith?
- Where do you turn when you have a question about the teaching of the Church?
- What is your most profound question about the Bible? About your Catholic faith?

Psalm Prayer

Psalm 146 (trust in God alone)

FIRST THEME: REVELATION AND FAITH

Life Connections

Here are some predictable attitudes and feelings that might arise for some, especially adults, during group conversations:

- Lack of confidence in their ability to understand the meaning of the Bible
- An experience of the "absence" of God at a difficult time
- Negative experiences connected with the sacrament of reconciliation

Introduction

Revelation is the name the church gives to the self-communication of God. Through revelation we learn of God's everlasting love for us and of our destiny to live forever with God. God's revelation was patient, gradual, and ever-powerful, as generations discovered that God was walking with and guiding them on their pilgrimage of faith.

God's revelation calls for the response of faith from each of us. Faith is the willing "yes" we make to God's offer of love and eternal happiness, and to all that God has revealed through Jesus Christ. In the four sessions that follow, believers of all ages will have the opportunity to learn more about God's revelation and to reflect upon their own faith response.

Session Topics

1. The Plan of Salvation

Seasonal Lectionary Connection: Year A

First Sunday of Advent

Isaiah 2:1–5 (the rule of Emmanuel)

Presentation Overview

God was first revealed to the Hebrew people as the one, true God. Gradually, men and women came to understand that they had a covenant relationship, both individually and as a people, with this one, personal God who gave them life and walked with them through all their joys and sorrows.

After the fall, God offered the hope of salvation to the first humans. Through succeeding generations, patriarchs, women of faith, prophets, and kings all contributed, through their various experiences, to the growing understanding of God. Many generations later, God was fully revealed through the life, death, and resurrection of Jesus Christ.

While our understanding of God's abiding presence continues to grow with the prompting of the Holy Spirit, there will be no further public revelation until the second coming of the Savior, when the reign of God will come in fullness. This session allows participants to reflect on the many ways in which God's revelation continues to touch our lives.

References: CCC, 50–53, 142, 143.

Dialogue Questions

- What aspect of God's revelation has touched you most deeply?
- Who has contributed most to your understanding of God and of God's son, Jesus Christ?
- What are you doing to make God's love more fully known to the world?

Psalm Prayer

Psalm 72 (the kingdom of the Messiah)

2. God Calls Us to Repentance

Seasonal Lectionary Connection: Year A

Second Sunday of Advent

Matthew 3:1–12 (John the Baptist prepares the way)

Presentation Overview

The more we learn of God, the more we are astounded by the extent to which God loves us. But we also confront our own failings and inadequacies before God's goodness and perfection. Every encounter with God is, then, a call to conversion and repentance.

John the Baptist sensed the imminent arrival of the Messiah whom God had promised through the ages. He summoned all who would listen to a baptism of water to signify repentance and conversion.

Ironically, John himself did not recognize at first that the promised

Redeemer was quite so close at hand. It was only through the power of the Spirit that the Baptist recognized that Jesus, his own cousin, was the promised one of God. Once he understood, John proclaimed to his death that Jesus was God's Son. This session challenges participants to consider their own need for deeper conversion to the Way of Jesus Christ.
References: CCC, 523, 535, 717–720.

Dialogue Questions

- When have you failed to notice the presence of God in your life?
- What experiences of your life have challenged you to deeper conversion?
- What role has the sacrament of reconciliation played in your faith journey?

Psalm Prayer
Psalm 109:1–9 (God, the savior of those in distress)

3. The Obedience of Faith

Seasonal Lectionary Connection: Year A

Fourth Sunday of Advent
Matthew 1:18–24 (Joseph responds in faith)

Presentation Overview
Obedience comes from a Latin word meaning "to hear or listen to." The obedience of faith, then, allows a person to hear fully the truth that God is revealing and to act accordingly. The story of Joseph, husband of Mary, is a vivid story of obedient faithfulness to God's call.

At first dismayed to learn that Mary is with child, Joseph obeys the message from God and takes Mary into his home and offers her his love and protection. His faith is so strong that it is able to overcome all the negative emotions he has felt on learning Mary's bewildering news. Joseph thus becomes an enduring example of faith.

In this third session, participants will have the opportunity to reflect upon the times when their faith, too, has been challenged by unexpected events, and the times when the grace of God and the help of the Holy Spirit have allowed them to trust and to respond in a positive way.

References: CCC, 144–165.

Dialogue Questions

- What other stories from the Bible have inspired you to deeper faith?
- When has it been hard to respond as obediently as Joseph did to a challenging call from God?
- Why is true obedience not in conflict with our human freedom?

Psalm Prayer

Psalm 27 (trust in God)

4. The Patience of Faith

Seasonal Lectionary Connection: Year A

Third Sunday of Advent

James 5:7–11 (on the patience of faith)

Presentation Overview

Today we live in a world of instant gratification. Television plots tie up neatly in an hour or less, relationships often begin and end at the whim of either party, "instant messaging" even intrudes as we answer an e-mail or search the internet. In fact, patience often seems an archaic word.

The author of the letter of James speaks specifically of the patience required of those oppressed by the wealthy. He asks his readers to recall the patience of the Hebrew prophets in the face of injustice, and reminds them of the reward to come for those who stand fast in the face of injustice and hardship. Implicit in his teaching is the church's preferential option, following the example of Jesus, to stand with and advocate for the needs of the poor.

James reminds us today that we cannot always see the outcome. Just as the farmer waits for the harvest, we, too, must sometimes wait for the mercy of God to be revealed. During Advent participants can reflect upon the patience that life can require. It is patience born of the faith that God's justice will ultimately prevail.

References: CCC, 2219, 2443-2448.

Dialogue Questions

- When have you felt frustrated or impatient with an unjust situation that you witnessed? What did you do about it?

- When were you patient with someone who did not act or respond as you wished?
- How are you helping make your family, your community, or the world a place of greater justice?

Psalm Prayer

Psalm 34 (the Lord protects the just)

SECOND THEME: THE INCARNATION OF GOD

Life Connections

Here are some predictable attitudes and feelings that might arise for some, especially adults, during group conversations:

- Lack of confidence in their ability to understand the meaning of the Bible, especially the Old Testament
- An experience of the "absence" of God at a difficult time
- Negative experiences connected with the sacrament of reconciliation
- A mistaken notion that salvation must be earned

Introduction

Jesus is the Son of God, conceived by the power of the Holy Spirit, and born of Mary. The mystery of the Incarnation, that Jesus is truly God and truly human, is one of the most profound truths of our Christian faith. Because Jesus brings to sinners the complete expression of God's relationship to all humanity, the church teaches that Jesus is the fullness of God's revelation.

This second theme focuses on Jesus as savior of all humanity, the redeemer who calls all believers to give witness "to the ends of the earth" to the good news he brings. Through the four sessions that follow, participants will have the opportunity to learn more about this mystery of faith and the ways in which it touches each human life.

Session Topics

1. The Announcement of the Messiah

Seasonal Lectionary Connection: Year A

Christmas: Midnight

Isaiah 9:1–6 (the Prince of Peace)

Presentation Overview

Christians believe that the Old Testament writings prefigure the coming of the Messiah in Jesus Christ. Yet the Old Testament has profound meaning in itself, for it, too, is the revelation of God. The church honors the Old Testament as the word of God, and God's covenant with the Hebrew people revealed there has never been revoked.

The book of Isaiah, particularly the messianic oracles, announces good news. The book incorporates writings by the great eighth-century prophet himself, but also those of his disciples, some of whom lived many years after him. Isaiah makes repeated references to Israel's deliverance from servitude and suffering by one who would be born into this world, upon whom the Spirit will rest. The Messiah will bring both judgment and justice, and then suffer, die, and be glorified by God.

While Isaiah and the other writers of these texts were writing in response to the suffering and injustice of their own times, Christians recognize a foreshadowing of Jesus Christ in these powerful poems. We read them with our knowledge of the life, death, and resurrection of Jesus. We see the Jesus of the New Testament as the fulfillment of Isaiah's words, "The people who walked in darkness have seen a great light" (Isaiah 9:1).

References: CCC, 127–133, 140.

Dialogue Questions

- When has knowing and believing the story of Jesus brought light into your life?
- When have you brought the light of Christ to another person? Who could use that light right now?
- What meaning do you see in the fact that God chose that the Messiah enter our world not as an earthly king, but as a vulnerable child?

Psalm Prayer

Psalm 96 (the kingship of Yahweh)

2. The Savior is Born

Seasonal Lectionary Connection: Year A

Christmas: Midnight

Luke 2:1–14 (the birth of Jesus)

Presentation Overview

Angels are always messengers with news of salvation. In Luke's gospel, the angel Gabriel directs Mary to name her son Jesus, which means "God saves." On the night of his birth, an angel of the Lord tells the shepherds that a savior has been born in Bethlehem. An angel tells Joseph to protect the infant Jesus by fleeing with his young family to Egypt.

Throughout his life, Jesus the savior reveals God's love and shows us how to act as the images of God that we are. Ultimately, by his death and resurrection, Jesus frees us from the bondage of sin and reconciles us with God. He does this by showing us, through his humanity, that it is possible to escape the effects of sin and live as children of light.

Salvation is the free gift of God; it is not something we can ever earn by our own merits. Nonetheless, a misuse of our human freedom could cause us to reject God's gift of eternal blessing. A proper use of freedom, rooted in profound gratitude, will always lead to liberation and to happiness. This incredible gift entered our world with the birth of a small child, Son of God and son of Mary.

References: CCC, 331–32, 456–81, 1739–42.

Dialogue Questions

- When has it been hard to remember the gift of salvation you have received?
- What can cause us to forget how much we are loved by God?
- Why are Christians called children of light?
- What is your definition of freedom?

Psalm Prayer

Psalm 97 (light dawns for the just)

3. Heirs of Christ

Seasonal Lectionary Connection: Year A

Feast of Mary, Mother of God

Galatians 4:4–7 (free sons of God in Christ)

Presentation Overview

St. Thomas Aquinas makes an astounding statement in one of his writings. "The only-begotten Son of God, wanting to make us sharers in his divinity, assumed our nature, so that he, made man, might make men gods" (*Opusculum*, 57:1–4). By responding to the gift of faith through our baptism and becoming disciples of Jesus Christ, we become adopted sons and daughters of God.

We know from the book of Genesis that we were created in the image and likeness of God. Original sin tarnished that likeness, and the sacrifice of Jesus Christ restored it. When we are anointed with the Holy Spirit at baptism, we become members of Christ's community and inherit the divine promise of salvation. We have the opportunity to conform ourselves more completely to the way of God's Son. This continuing conversion prepares our hearts to greet the God whose grace allows us to once again reflect the divine likeness.

References: CCC, 1701–09, 2784.

Dialogue Questions

- When have you felt most confident that your actions reflected the will of God?
- When have the good example and actions of others helped you grow in love?
- For whom are you trying to set a good example so that they will make good choices?

Psalm Prayer

Psalm 138 (hymn of a grateful heart)

4. We Proclaim the Savior

Seasonal Lectionary Connection: Year A

The Baptism of the Lord

Acts 10:34–38 (Peter's discourse)

Presentation Overview

Jesus Christ calls all believers to be witnesses to the truth, just as he was. Witnessing to our Christian faith has often been difficult for Catholics. Even when our faith is deeply held, we can be reticent about proclaiming it boldly to others. The first disciples themselves were afraid until the power of the Holy Spirit—a power given to us today through the sacraments—gave them the courage to speak.

St. Peter offers a vivid example of one who spoke with courage and the conviction of his faith in the Lord. In the Acts of the Apostles, his discourse to the Caesareans reveals two qualities of Christian witness. He speaks simply and eloquently, recounting the mighty deeds of Jesus of Nazareth. He also acknowledges a profound truth that he has come to understand—that salvation is offered to all people, without any partiality.

References: CCC, 857–65, 897–907.

Dialogue Questions

- Have you ever spoken openly to a non-Christian about your faith in Jesus Christ? Why or why not?
- What do you think is the most important thing about being a Christian?

Psalm Prayer

Psalm 145 (the greatness and goodness of God)

THIRD THEME: JESUS BRINGS GOD'S REIGN

Life Connections

Here are some predictable attitudes and feelings that might arise for some, especially adults, during group conversations:

- Resentment toward the poor whose burdens they bear
- Confusion, especially among younger adults, about the paradoxes of the beatitudes
- Feelings of unworthiness because of past mistakes, or self-satisfaction because of good choices

Introduction

The heart of Jesus' ministry is the announcement of the reign of God. When he stands in the synagogue and applies the words of the prophet Isaiah to himself, he reveals that his mission is to bring good news to the poor, set prisoners free, and proclaim a year of favor. He tells those present that on that very day, the ancient prophecy has been fulfilled.

Some were shocked by Jesus' words. Some felt he was arrogant, and others were simply bewildered. We can expect similar reactions when we act with selfless love toward others or speak the truth in ways that are completely unexpected.

Session Topics

1. The Lamb of God

Seasonal Lectionary Connection: Year A

Second Sunday in Ordinary Time

Isaiah 49:3, 5–6 (the servant of the Lord)
John 1:29–34 (John's testimony to Jesus)

Presentation Overview

Jesus' public life begins when John baptizes him in the river Jordan. The heavens that were closed with the sin of Adam are reopened, and the Spirit of God pours down once again. Jesus, the one who never sinned, did not require this water baptism. He submitted to it because of his love for us and his obedience to his Father. He would willingly experience the "baptism" of his passion one day at the hands of sinners so that we might be reborn to eternal life.

At that moment John the Baptist realized who Jesus really was and proclaimed him "the Lamb of God, who takes away the sin of the world" (John 1:29). He uses the image of the sacrificial lamb of the old covenant to announce the one who brings the new covenant. From that day forward, Jesus' entire life is one of poverty, obedience, service, and sacrifice. Disciples of Jesus are called to be servants of the message of Christ, just as he was the servant to all.

References: CCC, 536, 565, 608, 852, 876.

Dialogue Questions

- Which persons have given you the best examples of service and self-sacrifice? Why did you choose them?
- What is one way in which you have been of service to others?
- What does it mean to live in a spirit of poverty?

Psalm Prayer

Psalm 40 (gratitude and prayer for help)

2. The Ministry of Jesus

Seasonal Lectionary Connection: Year A

Third Sunday in Ordinary Time

Matthew 4:12–23 (the beginning of Jesus' ministry)

Presentation Overview

From the three synoptic gospel accounts, we know that Jesus began his public ministry with both words and actions. In Luke's gospel, he announces his mission in the synagogue of Nazareth, the town of his childhood. He proclaims that the Spirit of God is upon him, that God has sent him to bring good news to the poor and set captives free. Immediately, he travels about Galilee curing the sick and lame and casting out demons. In Matthew's gospel, Jesus' ministry begins immediately with acts of physical and spiritual healing.

The mission to the poor and suffering is at the heart of the gospel. The church speaks of a "preferential option for the poor" that all Christians are called to make, for it was the choice of Jesus and of his Father in heaven. The ministry of the baptized is to continue the mission of Jesus, and, armed with the power of the Spirit, to take responsibility for one another's needs and spread the gospel throughout the world.

References: CCC, 1716–1724, 1739–42, 1965–74.

Dialogue Questions

- What is your attitude or feeling toward the poor, or toward those who are physically or mentally challenged?
- When have you felt the need to be "set free"?
- In what ways have you taken on the mission of Jesus?

Psalm Prayer

Psalm 112 (the blessings of the just)

3. Jesus Describes the Reign of God

Seasonal Lectionary Connection: Year A

Fourth Sunday in Ordinary Time

Matthew 5:1–12 (the beatitudes)

Presentation Overview

The reign of God describes the time when the world will be completely restored to right standing, when peace and justice and joy will once again prevail. Jesus ushered in the reign of God. His life revealed what the fullness of God's reign would be. Through his actions and the power of the Spirit, the restoration of God's world is already underway.

The reign of God is a reality that is already present but not yet completely fulfilled. It exists whenever the people of God work for peace and justice, whenever we make the choice to love rather than to hate or exclude, and whenever we express joy, or gratitude, or forgiveness to one another. Throughout the gospels, Jesus provides images and actions to help us to understand the true path to happiness—choosing to live each day in the reign of God.

References: CCC, 535–7, 541–2, 876–79.

Dialogue Questions

- Where have you seen evidence in the world around you that God's reign is already present in the world?
- What images could you use to express to others what the reign of God is like?
- What are you doing to make God's reign more fully present?

Psalm Prayer

Psalm 146 (trust in God)

4. Challenges to Living in the Reign of God

Seasonal Lectionary Connection: Year A

Seventh Sunday in Ordinary Time

Matthew 5:38–48 (the demands of love)

Presentation Overview

We live in a world that often militates against the values of God's reign. Self-interest, greed, anger, betrayal, and retaliation often appear to have the upper hand. Even those who desire to live the values of the kingdom find themselves falling short. As Paul said, "I do not do what I want, but I do what I hate" (Romans 7:15). Which of us has not felt the same way from time to time?

Jesus constantly asks his followers to move beyond sin and toward goodness. His call is a radical one—not merely to avoid evil, but to live in a spirit of pure love and generosity. He asks us to give more than is required, to go out of our way to help others, to forgive even our enemies. Not all have been able to meet the demands of the gospel, but those who do are already living in the reign of God.

References: CCC, 547, 1849–51, 1939–42.

Dialogue Questions

- What have you done to overcome your disappointment when you have fallen short of your own goals for your Christian life?
- When do you feel you have done more than was required by the letter of the law to act in a Christian way?

Psalm Prayer

Psalm 62 (trust in God alone)

FOURTH THEME: LIFE IN CHRIST

Life Connections

Here are some predictable attitudes and feelings that might arise for some, especially adults, during group conversations:

- Misunderstandings about the difference between temptation and sin
- The feeling that salvation must be earned
- Reticence about acknowledging one's own virtues

Introduction

Morality is to live in Christ—to recognize that we have been brought from darkness and led by the light of Christ into the reign of God. Through faith, we recognize our fundamental human dignity as children of God and heirs of Christ's promise. Yet we also know that the power of evil still surrounds us and tempts us to betray the blessings we possess.

From the time of our first parents, we have seen that sin always begins with a temptation. Yet temptation in itself is not sinful. Even Jesus experienced temptation. It is only when we give in to temptation that we sin.

When we cooperate with the grace of God and practice the virtues we find it easier to resist temptation, avoid sin, and realize our Christian vocation. Disciples of Jesus look to him to observe the virtues in action. Jesus overcame temptation by remaining pure of heart. He never lost his focus on his Father in heaven. The Son of God became human to show us that virtuous living is possible for all.

Session Topics

1. Overcoming Temptation

Seasonal Lectionary Connection: Year A

First Sunday of Lent

Genesis 2:7–9, 3:1–7 (story of the fall)
Matthew 4:1–11 (the temptation of Jesus)

Presentation Overview

The book of Genesis holds the seeds of most, if not all, of the moral themes in the Bible. Certainly, the first three chapters of Genesis, with their stories of the creation of humans in God's image, humankind's fall from grace, and the hope of salvation offered by God, form the foundation for our understanding of the human condition. We are blessed by God, we sin, and yet God's love for us endures.

Adam and Eve are unable to resist the attraction to evil that we call temptation. Temptation can come from without or from within, but it always entices us to act selfishly and reject the love of God. Even Jesus was tempted but did not sin. He freely chose to remain obedient to his Father. By doing so, he showed us that we, too, can reject temptation and choose to do good. When we follow Jesus' example, pray as he did, and are open to the Spirit's gift of courage, we can accept the grace of God and choose to live in love.

References: CCC, 55, 289, 385–87, 538–40.

Dialogue Questions

- What helps you most to resist temptation and avoid sin?
- What are some sources of temptation in our world today? What can be done to eliminate these temptations?

Psalm Prayer

Psalm 34:12–23 (turn from evil and do good)

2. Redeeming Grace

Seasonal Lectionary Connection: Year A

Third Sunday of Lent

John 4:5–42 (the Samaritan woman at the well)

Presentation Overview

Before there was sin, there was grace. By grace we participate in the very life of God. Grace is also the help God gives us to choose the good and thereby accept the gift of eternal life. Grace is always a gift of the Father, given by Christ, through the power of the Holy Spirit.

Just as Adam was the source of sin in the world, Jesus is the source of grace. Jesus' life-giving power is clearly expressed in the story of the woman who meets Jesus at Jacob's well. Jesus offers her living water, which she comes to realize is more than a refreshing drink. Like water, grace refreshes the soul and gives life. The grace given through Christ redeems us from sin and makes possible our salvation.

References: CCC, 388, 1996–2005.

Dialogue Questions

- Why is living water such a good image for God's gift of grace? What other images could also help to describe this gift?
- Why do you think some people have trouble accepting the gift of God's grace?

Psalm Prayer

Psalm 92 (thanksgiving for God's fidelity)

3. Living with a Grateful Heart

Seasonal Lectionary Connection: Year A

Fourth Sunday of Lent

John 9:1–41 (the man born blind)

Presentation Overview

Gratitude for the gifts of life and salvation should stand at the heart of Christian living. Gratitude is a powerful virtue. The well-known Christian writer Robert Wicks has said that if we spent just two minutes a day in silence, solitude, and thanksgiving, our lives would be transformed.

The Eucharist we celebrate together each week is a profound act of gratitude. We bring our memory of all the blessings and healing of heart and mind that we have received. We offer prayers and signs of thanksgiving to the one from whom we receive all good things. We praise God's Son, who bestowed the gift of salvation. Through the power of the Christ event, the bread and wine we offer become once again the sacrificial body and blood of the Savior. When we leave the liturgy, we take the spirit of gratitude for the gift of salvation back to our homes, to our workplaces, and to our communities.

References: CCC, 1333–34, 1360, 1418.

Dialogue Questions

- When could you find two minutes a day to spend in silence, solitude, and thanksgiving?
- To whom do you most need to say "thank you" for your gift of faith?
- What will you be most grateful for when you celebrate Eucharist next Sunday?

Psalm Prayer

Psalm 138 (hymn of a grateful heart)

4. A Virtuous Life

Seasonal Lectionary Connection: Year A

Passion (Palm) Sunday

Philippians 2:6–11 (humility of Jesus)

Presentation Overview

In any human endeavor, good habits improve our performance. In business, everyone knows the importance of good work habits. In sports, we know that training, practice, and repetition of certain physical movements will improve our game.

The same is true of the moral life. Our souls, as well as our bodies, need practice in choosing the good, for it is not always easy to avoid sin in the pressure of the moment. The habits that prepare us to choose the good are called virtues. Making a particular virtue our own is a collaborative effort between God's helping grace and our own practice.

The theological virtues of faith, hope, and love make us God's children, able to receive the gift of eternal life. These virtues are infused directly by God. The four human virtues of prudence, justice, temperance, and fortitude are called the cardinal virtues, because they are the pivotal ones on which all the others hinge. Over a lifetime, practicing the virtues allows the love of God and neighbor to blossom in us and prepare us to receive the full blessings of eternal life.

References: CCC, 1803–1832.

Dialogue Questions

- Which virtues are most valued within your family?
- Whom do you admire as a person of virtue? Which virtues does this person reflect in his or her everyday life?
- Which virtue would you like to strengthen in yourself? Why?

Psalm Prayer

Psalm 101 (norms of life)

FIFTH THEME: CHRIST IS RISEN

Life Connections

Here are some predictable attitudes and feelings that might arise for some, especially adults, during group conversations:

- Frustration with disappointing experiences of the Eucharist
- Feelings of not being appreciated for sacrifices one has made
- Discomfort at imagining the risen Lord in those who are imperfect or irritating

Introduction

Just as Eucharist is the central sacrament, so the Easter season is the heart of the church's year. During the six weeks of Easter, we celebrate the triumph of the Lord over death and sin, and his bestowal of the grace of salvation on all who will accept it. Because each Eucharist also celebrates these saving events, Sunday is sometimes called a "little Easter."

Throughout the four sessions that follow, we will reflect upon the meaning of the paschal mystery. We'll explore the meaning of the Resurrection, the importance of memory, and the difference that faith in the Resurrection makes in the lives of service to which we are called.

Session Topics

1. Jesus, the Perfect Sacrifice

Seasonal Lectionary Connection: Year A

Holy Thursday

1 Corinthians 11:23–26 (the Lord's Supper)

Presentation Overview

When Americans go to Washington D.C., they often visit one of the memorials to past presidents and heroes—Lincoln, Jefferson, and the Vietnam or Korean veterans. These memorials remind us of deeds that reflect our highest national ideals. However, in the Judaeo-Christian tradition, memorial means much more.

In both the Jewish Passover feast and in the Eucharist, there is a sense that the event commemorated is both remembered and somehow made present again. Jews believe that the Exodus event marked not only their liberation from slavery in Egypt, but is their proof that God continues to live in their midst. Catholics believe that the crucifixion of Jesus celebrates the perfect sacrifice that liberated humans forevermore from the bondage of sin, and that it remains a living sacrifice today.

Through the proclamation of the Word and the Eucharistic meal, we bring our lives to the celebration, and recall there how we are meant to live. This is what it means to say that Eucharist is the source and summit of the Christian life.

References: CCC, 1324, 1354, 1362–1372.

Dialogue Questions

- When you are making a sacrifice for someone else, do you feel more free or less free? Why?
- How do you feel when someone goes out of his or her way to do something for you?
- What has been your best experience of Eucharist? What made it so?

Psalm Prayer

Psalm 116 (thanksgiving to God for help in need)

2. The Risen Lord

Seasonal Lectionary Connection: Year A

Easter Vigil

Mark 16:1–8 (the women at the tomb)

Presentation Overview

The resurrection of Christ was a real historical event. No one was present at the moment it happened, but reliable New Testament witnesses experienced the presence of Jesus, whom they had seen die, now alive among them. The resurrection was not a return to earthly life, for Jesus' risen body had moved to a plane beyond time and space. He appeared and disappeared at will by virtue of his divine power. His soul and body, separated by death, have now returned to a perfect unity.

Jesus pledged to his followers that each human body would also rise one day. When Jesus raised believers such as Lazarus back to life, he offered each of us a sign of our destiny. Yet, in a sense, Christians have already risen with

Christ. For through our baptism in the Holy Spirit and our celebration in Eucharist, we already share in the death and resurrection of Christ.

References: CCC, 638–55, 992–96, 1168–71.

Dialogue Questions

- In what way does belief in the resurrection of Jesus make your life different from that of non-believers?
- What could you do to heighten your celebration of the Sunday Eucharist?

Psalm Prayer

Psalm 16 (God the supreme Good)

3. Recognizing the Lord

Seasonal Lectionary Connection: Year A

Second Sunday of Easter

John 20:19–31 (appearance to the disciples)

Presentation Overview

The various gospel accounts and the letters of Paul attest to appearances of the risen Christ before his ascension to heaven: first to the women at the tomb, then to the Twelve, and then to other disciples. Some who encounter Jesus recognize him immediately. Others, like Thomas, take longer to recognize and believe that Jesus is truly alive.

In his risen body, Jesus was able to appear in other guises familiar to them in order to awaken their faith. Thus he suddenly appears in a locked room and asks the doubting Thomas to place his hands in his wounds and his side.

Jesus Christ lives among us today. Yet, as Mother Teresa said, he often presents himself to us in most distressing disguises—often among the poor, the marginalized, the imprisoned, even among those who seem spiritually lost. As Christians, we try to recognize him and respond as he did, with love. All the sacraments of the church celebrate the risen Christ among us and strengthen us for this work.

References: CCC, 638–55, 992–96, 1168–71.

Dialogue Questions

- When have you been challenged to see the risen Lord in a surprising place?

- What barriers keep you from responding to the needs of others as you wish you could?

Psalm Prayer

Psalm 118 (hymn of thanksgiving to the savior of Israel)

4. Bread for Others

Seasonal Lectionary Connection: Year A

Feast of the Body and Blood of Christ

John 6:51–58 (the living bread)

Presentation Overview

As we hear in the Eucharistic Prayer, the bread and wine used there signify the fruit of the earth and "the work of human hands." As the bread is broken and the wine is consumed, we ritualize once more who Jesus is for the world and who we are to be. Jesus is the living bread sent by the Father, and we are to be the same for others.

Each time we pray the Our Father, we ask God to "give us this day our daily bread." We recognize in those words both our dependence on our Creator and the challenge to share our loaf with many, by serving those in need and working constantly for justice.

As St. Ignatius of Loyola said, "Pray as if everything depended on God, and work as if everything depended on you." Those, especially, who have celebrated the sacraments of holy orders or Christian marriage, or who have professed vows in religious life, bind themselves in service to one another and to all the people of God. However, all Christians share in this priesthood by virtue of their baptism.

References: CCC, I133–1336, 1342–43, 1406.

Dialogue Questions

- To what special work for the kingdom of God do you feel called right now?
- What is the greatest challenge to your vocation right now? How are you strengthening yourself to meet this challenge?

Psalm Prayer

Psalm 15 (the guest of God)

SIXTH THEME: THE CHURCH, LIGHT OF HUMANITY

Life Connections

Here are some predictable attitudes and feelings that might arise for some, especially adults, during group conversations:

- Among older parishioners, negative images of church from their childhood
- Resentment toward new ethnic groups moving into what may have been a more homogeneous parish
- Discomfort over taking an active role in the church's mission

Introduction

The church continues the ministry of Christ to bring the reign of God into the world. Each member of the church has the responsibility to continue this work of bringing God's love, peace, and justice to all.

In this series, participants will explore the nature of the church's mission, the central importance of the message of God's forgiveness, and the mandate to bring the good news to all people, without exception. Finally, they will examine the responsibility of each Christian to discover his or her vocation and to place it at the service of the church.

Session Topics

1. The Church's Mission

Seasonal Lectionary Connection: Year A

Feast of Pentecost

Acts 2:1–13 (the descent of the Holy Spirit)

Presentation Overview

The church is the gathering together of the people of God. The earthly form of the church began remotely when God promised Abraham that he would be the father of a great nation. Her foreshadowing continued with the election of Israel as the people of God.

In the fullness of time, God's Son announced the good news of the reign of God and gathered a family of disciples around him. It was to this "little flock" that the Spirit was sent at Pentecost, empowering the spread of the gospel to all peoples. That is why we often speak of Pentecost as the "birthday of the church."

By sending his Spirit to them, Christ proclaimed that the people of God had now become his body on earth. This body of Christ is one, holy, catholic, and apostolic. The church is one because her source is in the Trinity of Persons revealed to us by Jesus Christ. This one source, particularly the indwelling of the Spirit, makes the church ever holy. Saints also give witness to the holiness of the church.

The church is catholic because she exists wherever Christ is, and also because her mission is to the whole human race. All baptized Christians share in this mission of evangelization. She is apostolic because she is founded and still led by the spirit and teaching authority of the Apostles and their successors today. The church is on a pilgrimage, and will only reach perfection with the coming of the fullness of the reign of God at the end of history.

References: CCC, 751–768, 813–65.

Dialogue Questions

- When did you first become aware that you were a part of the worldwide people of God?
- In what way are you taking part in the church's mission?
- How does your membership in the church affect the way you live day by day?

Psalm Prayer

Psalm 105 (God's fidelity to his promise)

2. The Gospel of Forgiveness

Seasonal Lectionary Connection: Year A

Twenty-fourth Sunday in Ordinary Time

Matthew 18:21–35 (the merciless official)

Presentation Overview

The church is a light to the nations. Her mission is to reflect Christ, the light of the world, just as the moon reflects the sun. All of us who are members are called to reflect Christ's light by proclaiming and living the good news of salvation. Part of the light we shed on the world is Jesus' gospel of forgiveness.

The forgiveness of sins is an article of faith that we proclaim each week in the Nicene Creed. This message is at the heart of the good news of Jesus. The gospels are filled with stories of Jesus' willingness to put aside the sins of those who expressed repentance. The merciless official Jesus speaks of in Matthew's gospel has gratefully accepted his master's forgiveness but is not willing to bestow the same gift on one indebted to him. Jesus tells this story to impress upon us that our mission is to forgive others as he forgave, "not seven times; I say seventy times seven" (Matthew 18:22).

We admit our sinfulness and God's forgiveness each time we pray the Our Father. Through the church, we have the gift of the sacrament of reconciliation to ask for and receive God's forgiveness and to celebrate our ongoing conversion of heart. We then take the gift of our own forgiveness and share with others, through words and actions, our faith in the forgiveness that is available to all.

References: CCC, 976–983, 1449–1449, 2227.

Dialogue Questions

- To what extent could your family be called a school of forgiveness?
- When is forgiveness hard, and when is it easy?

Psalm Prayer

Psalm 103 (praise of divine goodness)

3. All Are Welcome

Seasonal Lectionary Connection: Year A

Twentieth Sunday in Ordinary Time

Matthew 15:21–28 (the faith of the Canaanite woman)

Presentation Overview

The church is leaven to the world. She brings the good news to all who are open to hear it. Bringing the message of Jesus Christ to a new culture requires a willingness to inculturate the message in the people to whom it is presented.

Just as Jesus adapted himself to the social and cultural circumstances of the people among whom he lived, the church today must adapt itself respectfully to new cultures so that hearts can be touched deeply by the gospel message. For example, the Rite of Christian Initiation of Adults allows for the incorporation of local rituals into the initiation rites. This process of inculturation acknowledges that the different traditions and devotions of other cultures express the unique spiritualities of different peoples and places.

When missionaries approach members of another culture, they do so in a spirit of respectful dialogue, appreciating the elements of truth and grace that are already there. This diversity is one of the greatest riches of the worldwide church.

References: CCC, 849–854, 1200–1206, 1232, 2684.

Dialogue Questions

- In what ways has your parish been enriched by the presence of members of different cultures?
- Which devotion or religious tradition treasured by your family is a part of your cultural background?

Psalm Prayer

Psalm 47 (the Lord, the king of all the nations)

4. Using Our Gifts

Seasonal Lectionary Connection: Year A

Thirty-third Sunday in Ordinary Time

Matthew 25:14–30 (the parable of the silver pieces)

Presentation Overview

The servants in the parable of the silver pieces were asked to maximize the funds they were given according to their abilities. In the same way, each of us is given gifts and talents that God calls us to develop to the fullest extent we are able. St. Paul reminds us that the gifts are rich and varied, but something is given to each of us.

We receive these gifts in order to build up the reign of God. The way we use them is what we mean by our Christian vocation. Through the power of the Holy Spirit, we use them first of all to become holy and to bring the message of Christ to the world. We also choose a path in life that allows us the greatest use of our gifts—the ordained priesthood, religious life, marriage, or the committed single life.

At baptism, each of us was anointed priest, prophet, and king. As priest, we take the sacrifices of everyday life and consecrate them as we offer them in worship. As prophet, we accept our mandate to bear witness to the truth and to lead others to faith in Jesus Christ. As king, we exercise our power as children of God first to bring our own desires and passions into obedience to the one in whom we believe. We also work to conform the structures of society to the gospel of justice.

References: CCC, 898–913, 1533, 1992, 2030.

Dialogue Questions

- What do you consider to be your Christian vocation?
- How are you fulfilling the mandate?

Psalm Prayer

Psalm 40 (gratitude and prayer for help)